Follow your Dream into the Wind —

OLD FLORIDA

ISBN: 1546430407
ISBN-13: 978-1546430407

21st CENTURY CHALLENGE:

PRESERVING NATIVE FLORIDA

Nancy Dale, Ph.D.

COVER PHOTO

MARVIN KAHN

FOUNDER OF "FLORIDA CRACKER TRAIL"

AND

KAHN CITRUS MANAGEMENT LLC

OTHER BOOKS BY NANCY DALE

ORDER INSCRIBED BOOKS:

NANCYDALEPHD@GMAIL.COM

Where the Swallowtail Kite Soars:
The Legacies of Glades County, Florida and the Vanishing Wilderness
ISBN: 0-595-32557-2

Would Do, Could Do and Made Do:
Florida's Pioneer Cow Hunters Who Tamed the Last Frontier
ISBN: 0-595-41568-7

Wild Florida The Way It Was As Told by the Florida Pioneer "Cow Hunters" Who Lived It
ISBN: 0-595-51104-4

The Legacy of the Florida Pioneer "Cow Hunters" - In Their Own Words
ISBN: 978-1-4502-8789-0

Deadly Risk:
American Cattle Ranching on the Mexican Border and Other True Cattle Ranching Stories
ISBN: 978-1-4921-5523-2

FISHEATING CREEK AND CYPRESS TREE

DEDICATION

"This book is dedicated to the reader to engage in Life in all its NATURAL Beauty, as it is now and as it was, with the Freedom to enjoy it every day on an endless basis."

Jim Hendrie, Venus, Florida

Dairyman, Cattle Rancher - Member of

the Lake Placid Rotary Club

And

To Gregory Lasanta for Awakening me to Life!

Wash Morgan 1900 Chuck Wagon cook on the cattle drives

PREFACE

April 27, 2017

Florida is unique. The old days of Florida will never return but the true stories of the people who lived it, as in the other books, are preserved forever.

The living future is yet to be written.

JOHN PLATT

ZOLFO SPRINGS

ACKNOWLEDGEMENTS

Writing a book is an exploration into the unknown. It is an adventuresome journey through unexpected twists and turns. This book tells the true stories of Floridians preserving and creating a new Florida.

The gracious people herein, reveal their dreams, hopes, beliefs and goals as they accept and act upon the 21st Century Challenge: Preserving Native Florida.

With great humility, I am fortunate to have been invited into their lives and their living legacy.

A generous "Thank You" to Jennifer Swain, Editor. Her tireless effort, valuable objective evaluations have been vital in completing this project. This book is a shining reflection of her talent and potential.

Additionally, I appreciate the contributions of Judy Crisp who helped to move this project forward, as she did through the completion of my other books. I am grateful!

Thank you Marsha and Larry Taylor, owners of the Palmdale Store and James Sprague, former General Manager for a wonderful year before the Store's last breath of life. Your contributions are a tribute to Palmdale's legacy.

Inspiring leadership to create the Future, Steve Jobs, Apple Computer, addressed a graduating class at Stanford University with these insightful words:

"Your time is limited, so don't waste it living someone else's

> ***life. Don't be trapped by dogma living with the results of other people's thinking."***

Thus, I present the lives of these Floridians not "trapped by dogma," manifesting their Dreams for our Future.

Nancy Dale, Ph.D.
January 2017

CONTENTS

SUNRISE IN LORIDA OVER THE KISSIMMEE RIVER

PHOTO BY: JENNIFER SWAIN

FORWARD

BY

COLONEL CHARLES T. HEBERLEE III RUSSIAN FEDERATION PROGRAM

"Tradition" vs. "Progress," an ancient debate as old as Time always surrounded by controversy whether in Florida or the Antarctic.

Every atom in the universe is always in motion; there is not one second when everything is the same as before. "Progress" is inevitable and, if balanced with tradition, is usually for "the good". "Tradition," on the other hand, exists in the human mind and spirit coveted with emotional attachments. Our duty in the community is to take responsibility for both and ensure that progress doesn't trample upon "Tradition". In this book, "The 21st Century Challenge of Preserving Native Florida, Nancy is tackling this concern through the lives of people who are preserving valued traditions in times of change and "progress."

The question to ask: Where and when do we stop and consider where we are going before rushing off into the unknown, unpredictable future? The first step in finding direction is to use a map to determine where we are and to figure out where we are going before we strike out on a new course.

Does progress mean that we must give up our emotional ties to the past? If we save something are we emotionally attached to such as a way of life, pristine piece of land, historic building or are we standing in the way of progress? I remember one time when I was at a meeting to decide if a particular "art deco" theater was to be designated a historic building. One of the

Historical Commission Members was late to the meeting. While waiting, the Commission Chairman talked about the difficulty of deciding what was truly "historical" and worth saving. She said, "I ask myself all the time if something which was built in my lifetime is truly historical or am I just emotionally attached to it and does that mean it should be spared from the progress of development such as more housing? We must be prepared to make this same value judgment regarding proposed "progress" everywhere as "creeping urbanization" engulfs the land, the wilderness and the wildlife.

If we let emotion rule the day, the more powerful emotion of making money will probably win. "Progress" and "Success" are often measured by how much financial return results rather than the greater good for the community. "MEP" - Money, Ego and Power are forces that often masquerade as "progress" but rarely deliver it. It is always good when investigating and deciding on whether to "progress" to ask three questions:

- *What is the purpose of this "progress"?*
- *Who benefits and how?*
- *Is money, ego and power the primary factor?*
- *Does the project do the greatest good for the greatest number?*

Even the fact that "progress" may disrupt peoples' lives is a fact that can factor into the argument. The classic American principle is to do the greatest good for the greatest number. It is a key philosophy in a successful Democracy.

It is my hope that those of you reading this book will stand for principled investigation before plundering in the future. We need to keep our eyes open for a public hearing, to be informed and do research; we may also have our own "public hearing" with neighbors to discuss what issues we need to uphold for the common good. If there is an issue of concern, come prepared to an official public hearing with a group position, facts and pro-active communication skills; it will change everything. If a group comes with a reasoned position, it will be a factor and a point to be seriously considered in case of legal proceedings.

However, start here. Be inspired by those who have lived their lives carving their own lifestyles. Determine what is predicted as "inevitable" and how it should be dealt with such as Florida's "build-out" and can each of us make a difference to protect the natural Beauty bestowed upon the dwellers here in Florida before it turns to concrete.

So we are back to "Progress" vs."Tradition". Both good things in their place. But, what is important in the 21st Century Florida are issues we each must decide then determine our actions. It is up to us, not a government or large corporate entity, to decide how we choose to live. We all can be part of progress in the human condition. We are a Democracy and we need to preserve it.

Colonel Charles T. Heberlee III, BA and MA,
Created and established a program by and for the Russian Federation to change the minds of their people from "Subject" to "Citizen" over the next generation.

Author: You the People Handbook for Citizens Action Group Members and "Student Citizenship Training Program" taught in 3,000 high schools nationwide and overseas.

ONE

"LIVING LEGEND OF THE FLORIDA CITRUS INDUSTRY AND FOUNDER OF THE "CRACKER TRAIL"

MARVIN KAHN
SEBRING

When I snapped Marvin Kahn's picture standing in front of a giant mural of Mike and Sadie Kahn, his parents, painted on a wall in downtown Sebring, Florida, I knew I was looking at a legend. I observed the pride in Marvin Kahn's eyes, voice and gestures as he began to tell his family's story, weaving through early American history to the place where we were now standing at the "Sadie Kahn Memorial Park". The Kahn family story brings chills to the body and admiration for a man who manifested his dreams in seemingly insecure, impossible times; however, with perseverance and faith in his dreams shared with many others, they became reality.

Marvin Kahn was the fourth child born in Sebring to Sadie and Mike "Kovalski." The Kovalski's were Lithuanian Jewish immigrants who came to America via Ellis Island between 1920-1926. Mike Kovalski was on a boat coming to America when World War I broke-out. Mike's older brother, Barney, had previously entered the United States sponsored by a cousin living in Atlanta. When he arrived at Ellis Island, the family name was changed to "Kahn."

Marvin Kahn recalls the stories his mother told him about living in Lithuania when it was under Russian, Poland, Lithuanian rule. "There was very limited freedom in Lithuania as Jews were deprived of owning a business, getting an education and employment was very limited. When Jewish boys turned 13 years of age, they were drafted into the Russian Army. However, before World War I, life in Lithuania under German rule in Germany was much better for Jews. Jews prospered with personal freedom. This caused a significant number of Jews to migrate into Germany from all over Eastern Europe. However, with the onset of World

Word II and Hitler's Holocaust, Jews became the 'scapegoat'. With severe deprivation in post-World War I Germany, Hitler's untruths began to spread and were believed by the non-Jewish German population. Six million Jews were massacred," Kahn explains.

Marvin Kahn's daddy, Mike Kahn, followed in his brother's footsteps to Georgia where he and wife, Sadie settled in Sales City. Kahn says, "Mamma did not like her new home as she said it reminded her of Lithuania, so daddy decided to look elsewhere. He hitched a ride with a truck driver to an unknown place he heard about called 'Avon Park, Florida'. After looking around, he asked about other nearby towns and was told about a new one: 'Sebring, Florida', a few miles south." Kahn began to walk south in that direction.

As an enterprising man, Kahn was looking for a business opportunity, a pleasing town for Sadie and a happy place to start over in America. When he arrived in Sebring, he met the town's founder, George E. Sebring and talked to him about opening a dry goods business downtown. Mr. Sebring offered Kahn a retail location in a new building under construction, the Nancesowee Hotel, a building site next to the lot that Kahn eventually donated in honor of his parents: “The Sadie Kahn Memorial Park.

The inscription reads:

SADIE KAHN MEMORIAL PARK

HIGHLANDS COUNTY IS A SUBTROPICAL PARADISE WHERE GEORGE SEBRING FOUNDED A NEW TOWN IN 1912. IN 1923 MR. SEBRING WELCOMED MIKE AND SADIE KAHN & A STRONG FRIENDSHIP FORMED. THEY OPENED A STORE ON RIDGEWOOD DR. & MR. SEBRING GAVE MIKE A LOT FOR A SYNAGOGUE. MIKE BOUGHT HIS FIRST GROVE & HOME ON OLD DESOTO CITY RD. & THE KAHN'S CITRUS INTERESTS BLOSSOMED. THIS SADIE KAHN MEMORIAL PARK WAS NAMED BY THE CITY IN 1980 AND WAS REDEDICATED FOR SEBRING'S CENTENNIAL IN 2012. KENNETH TREISTER DESIGNED THE CENTENNIAL SCULPTURES & BENCHES.

By 1933, the dry goods business had prospered and Mike expanded his interest purchasing his first citrus grove. “Citrus” was an interest he had learned in Lithuania living amongst non-Jewish farmers when he was not allowed to own land. To this day, Marvin Kahn says, “some of the original trees are still alive in his groves.” When Marvin Kahn was 10 years old his daddy passed away but by then he had accumulated 200 acres of citrus as a grower and business man.

As the family business thrived, Marvin Kahn decided he wanted to follow his longtime dream of becoming a cattle rancher and citrus man. He attended Sebring High School, joined the 4-H Club and met lifelong friend, later, State Legislator, Burt Harris. “When I was young, I didn’t have the foresight to learn what I could have learned in the cattle business as I learned everything on my own. I didn’t know anything about marketing which is important in the cattle industry today,” says Kahn.

“Utilizing my University of Florida education, I experimented with a piece of land in South Lake Placid on Highway 70. It was a sand hill with muck that needed drainage and sand.” He added with a chuckle, "The land was so poor that 'a rabbit would need to carry his lunch'. However, this does not agree with the current thinking about the land's potential. I sold the parcel to my friend Bert Harris and now it is it planted in beautiful citrus," boasts Kahn.

In the meantime, Kahn had another inspiration. This new idea was spawned by the "Woodpecker Trail", "Soul of the South," Highway 121 from Gainesville, Florida to Charlotte, North Carolina. The "Woodpecker Trail" carried travelers from South Carolina and Georgia to Florida. The "Woodpecker Trail" was a marketing idea to draw people back into Florida's interior.

Kahn's inspiration was to commemorate Florida's 200-year heritage of the cattle industry with the creation of a Florida Cracker Trail. In the 1800s as ranchers migrated into Florida, they bred their herds with Andalusian cattle left behind by Ponce de Leon. Historical records reveal that Florida then had vast swamps and flatlands of pine and oak proving to be ideal for the development of ranches with the Government offering economic incentives to settle the land. Many southerners trailed into Wild Florida, an unknown rugged destination of struggle and an attitude of 'survival-of-the-fittest' just like the pioneer Indians before them," says Kahn.

In the 1800s, cattle were herded across Florida to Punta Rassa on the West coast where they were shipped by riverboat to Cuba after the Spanish American War to replenish the beef supply and out of Ft. Pierce, on the east coast, they were shipped throughout the breadbasket of the world. Kahn says, "Florida's pioneer 'cow hunters' carved a path into Florida or poled through deep swamps with the family stowed on wooden wagons, cattle and dogs tramping alongside, forging into Florida after three Seminole Indian Wars. Two hundred years ago, a new page in Florida history was beginning to be recorded."

Kahn wanted the replication of the old "Cracker Trail" to be an annual calling to ranchers to honor the legendary "cow hunters".

Kahn felt that the Florida Cracker Trail should run along a route from Fort Myers on the west coast to Ft. Pierce on the east coast.

In 1955, Pershing Platt of Hardee County was instrumental in the creation of the Cracker Trail Association. He first rode a horse on the original Cracker Trail when he was 15 years old and was also the first trail boss on the first trail ride along with many others from all over the state.

"It was my wife, Elsa, who asked an artist friend to create the now famous emblem of the Florida Cracker Trail Association. The design depicts the cross-state trail with a cowboy on his horse swinging the ever-present, utilitarian cracker whip used to keep cattle in check on the long cattle drives and send messages to other cowboys miles up the line.

The emblem today symbolizes the Florida Cracker Trail Association. The Florida Cracker Trail Association (FCT) yearly ride crosses Central Florida through miles of orange groves on State Road 64, 66 and County Road 68.

As Kahn talked to me about the "Cracker Trail", I accompanied him on a drive west on State Road 66 from Sebring to the "first ranch where I was a 'cowboy'," says Kahn. Today, the remains of his Crewsville ranch with horse stable and deteriorating feed trough has been incorporated into the Florida Cracker Trail.

Kahn's own legacy covers a history of eighty-three years from cowboy to businessman and leader in the Florida citrus industry. Today, he has taken on a major concern of citrus growers across the state, the devastating "citrus greening".

As I arrived at a long metal building displaying a sign reading: Kahn Citrus Management, LLC and Murphy Agriculture Solutions of the Heartland, LLC, the building was almost lost in the vestige of an old Sebring revival neighborhood beneath the tower of a deserted power plant. Except for the bright welcoming yellow awnings, I might have missed the new offices that Kahn and his 27-year-old partner, Trevor Murphy, occupy as they forge ahead into the innovate science of healing deadly citrus greening threatening to destroy Florida Citrus of all kinds.

Opening into a spacious office, I was greeted by two friendly ladies who have worked for Kahn many years: India Craske and Angel Nowling. I relinquished my imagination from the long pathway of Kahn's past into a Vision of Hope in their promising endeavor and the future of Kahn's lifelong calling in the citrus groves. Kahn's philosophy is always focused on moving forward to make "improvement in all regards" and now he faces a crucial challenge.

"A major concern in the citrus industry today is the cost to expand

and make all necessary improvements. The largest most expensive improvement is a cure or a way to live and make money dealing with citrus greening. Citrus greening is a devastating disease and if no effort is made to improve our citrus trees, they will all die! There are efforts moving forward to improve the present crop by reducing stress, drought and disease of the trees. Improving the health of existing trees by reducing their size to induce juvenile trees for production is important and a good use of 'time', the biggest and most expensive cost for making improvements," Kahn expresses with concern. "A very big help, in this regard, is planting new citrus groves. The new IRS rule has recently changed to allow the cost of planting to be 'expensed' rather than amortizing the cost over five years; a very significant improvement. Florida Citrus Mutual Manager, Mike Sparks is implementing this change with Congress", Kahn emphasizes.

Citrus Greening is bacteria transmitted by the African citrus psyllid that stunts the growth of trees. The disease was first reported in China in 1943 but was known to exist since the 20's in South

Africa and worldwide. Kahn says that "greening affects the leaves that support the roots, damages the fruit and the tree eventually dies. In Florida, today, citrus crop production has gone down 30 to 40% a year." Kahn and Murphy are working with the Citrus Research and Educational Foundation (CREF) to find a way to save the trees. "It is still a mystery on how to solve the problem but we have to have profitable production of a citrus tree with youthful vitality and vigor to fight off the bacteria. The industry cannot survive without economic growth, people and supplies. We have to find a way to live with the infestation. Our business model is to search for a way to produce healthy trees, giving water when the trees need moisture, protecting them from stress, drought, floods and bugs. We are currently working with scientists from universities to discuss a new direction. We have no choice but to find a solution to inhibit greening for profitable citrus tree production." "This is our Mission", emphasizes Kahn. "'Time' is the biggest cost to use wisely."

Marvin Kahn's career is as large as ever as he moves into the

21stCentury focusing on innovative methodologies to revive the citrus industry by solving the immediate catastrophe for its survival in the future.

CRACKER TRAIL RIDE – FORT PIERCE

TWO

"AFTER THE RIDE" TRAIL GATHERING

CROOKED BAR RANCH, SEBRING

ELSA AND MARVIN KAHN

It was a beautiful Saturday as the sun glanced through tall oaks shading a stream of more than 50 riders on the "After Ride" trail gathering at the Crooked Bar Ranch in Sebring. This event celebrates the 30th Annual 110 mile Florida Cracker Trail Ride across the state which occurred February 18-21st starting in Bradenton and ending at Bud Adam's ranch Fort Pierce.

"Keeping history alive every step of the way," the first Cracker Trail ride took place in 1987 and has attracted thousands of riders the world over to commemorate Florida's cattle ranching heritage. It was Sebring cowboy/citrus grove owner/Manager, Marvin Kahn's inspiration to celebrate Florida's 200 year heritage with the founding of the Cracker Trail Ride and Association.

Back in the saddle again on this Saturday, Marvin Kahn, sits tall on Trail Boss's Suzanne Park's horse, "Willow" accompanied by her two daughters, Isabella and Reagan. Kahn headed the pack curving into his old Crooked Bar Ranch founded in 1955, now part of the Cracker Trail. It was two days filled with fun and memories.

The Cracker Trail Ride and After Ride bring together riders of all ages, experience, and horse breeds. Majestically prancing through the gates, hardly recognized as a "mule," Marilyn Whitford, Jacksonville was saddled up on "Dolly," a cross between a donkey and horse whose early breeding dates back in the U.S. to 1785 when George Washington asked King Charles of Spain for a donkey to breed mules as work animals on his Mount Vernon plantation. Donkeys date back 3000 B.C. in Egypt to the Pharaohs.

Entertaining the folks as they cleaned up after the ride, dropped hay and fed horses was little Jared Harrison, Myakka City, having fun in the middle of a field taking time to perfect his skills at the cracker whip. He started to learn the intricate twists, turns and clever cracks as early as four years old mimicking techniques that were originally used to keep cattle in check along the long stretches of the original cattle drives.

After riders and horses settled down awaiting a delicious hot barbecue pot luck, laughs and "tall tales" about the last ride, Marvin and Elsa Kahn stopped by to chat with Sheila Taylor brushing down her beautiful "Pantalusa" horse that the author had the opportunity to mount pretending to be riding "bare back."

The history of the Florida Cracker Trail dates back to the 1800s, as ranchers migrated into Florida, breeding their herds with Andalusian cattle left behind by Ponce de Leon in the 1500's. Florida then had vast swamps and flatlands, ideal for the development of ranches when the Government offered economic incentives to settle the land. Kahn says, "It took an attitude of "survival-of-the-fittest." The original cracker trail was carved as cattle were herded to markets across Florida to Punta Rassa on the west coast and Ft. Pierce on the east coast.

Kahn wanted the replication of the old "Cracker Trail" to be an annual calling of ranchers to honor legendary "cow hunters" who gathered cattle for shipment to market that were running wild in the scrub before fence laws. Pershing Platt was the first Trail Boss and Elsa Kahn asked an artist to create the now famous emblem of the Florida Cracker Trail Association, depicting a cowboy on his horse swinging the utilitarian cracker whip.

At the finish of the present day "After Ride," it was time for laughs and memories to be preserved until next year when it all begins again. Riders will convene, horses will gleam, and excitement will brew as everyone looks forward to another year of camaraderie and history.

THREE

THE 21st ANNUAL JUNIOR CYPRESS CATTLE DRIVE AND RODEO

A NEW GENERATION OF YOUNG COWBOYS/COWGIRLS

It was a beautiful, sunny day when the young riders, girls and boys, ages 4 through 18 saddled up their horses and rode into a day of adventure at the Big Cypress Seminole Reservation's 21th Annual Junior Cypress Cracker Trail Ride and Eastern Indian Rodeo Association (EIRA) event at the Jr. Cypress Arena.

In the pristine wilderness of Hendry County, the trail ride started at the western boundary of the Big Cypress traveling down Country Road 833 to the arena. Leading the pack of riders was one of this year's Honorary Trail Bosses, Paul Bowers with a tribute also to Honorary Trail Boss, Morgan Smith (deceased). Many other riders joined in on the excitement riding their own horses while other visitors rode the parade route packed into the Billy Swamp Safari swamp buggy with beautiful Junior Miss Rodeo, Gladios Yanos, riding up front smiling and waving to spectators.

When the entourage of horseback riders, passengers, turned into the rodeo arena, fans hooped and hollered in anticipation of the upcoming events. Greeting visitors on her horse "Jack," waiting to enter the arena was Eastern Indian Rodeo Association Queen, Allegra Billie. It was a day to be remembered by young "seasoned" cowboys and visitors.

Moses Juniper enthusiastically announced the day's action as rodeo chutes were thrown open and crowds held their breath watching young cowboys/cowgirls with high hopes leap into the arena tightly holding onto their reigns for the 6 second ride. Even though some young pros were thrown off as powerful hooves landed all around them, the youthful contenders got, dusted themselves off and proudly walked away to the fans applauds.

Seventy kids, ages 7 through 17, participated in everything from calf roping to steer riding. Some of the helmeted youth were just learning how to ride with one hand like the big cowboys. Four-year-old, Dale Gorney bravely participated in the mutton busting ride while Justin Rodriguez took first place. Another young rider, Kayle Alex rose to first place in the 4 to 8-year-old Barrel Racing Event as well as taking first place in the 7-9 category of Youth Pony Riding. Alex Rodriguez, gained 34 points to take First Place in that division as well as in the 7-10-year-old Youth Calf Riding.

Chucky Osceola won first place in the 10-12-year-old category of Youth Pony Riding and took another first place in the 11-13-year-old Youth Steer Riding event.

The Chute Doggin' contest, where a rider sits in the chute atop a steer instead of a horse, Austin Thomas took first place and won

first place in Break Way Roping while Madison Osceola won the top prize in the 8-17-year-old category. As the more experienced riders took center stage in the 9-12 age group, Madison Jumper breathlessly won first place and Madison Osceola took the win in the 13-27 age group. All the winners took home prize money for their talented performances.

Justin Gopher, Senior was the event Judge and Melissa Gopher helped to keep score of the winners and cash prizes for those riding up to 6 seconds in each event. Inside the tent area, near the arena, guests enjoyed having BBQ lunch and a slice of "Junior Cypress" cake to the accompaniment of Paul Buster's songs and guitar. The full day of activities included a breakfast, BBQ dinner and a night rodeo for the seasoned riders.

The story of the Junior Cattle Drive originated in 1997 when the first Seminole cattle drive was held in conjunction with the 2nd Annual Junior Cypress Rodeo. The idea of the Junior Trail Ride was the inspiration of Moses Jumper Jr., Paul Bowers Sr. and Richard Bowers. Replicating the Florida Cattle Drive across Central Florida inspired by Marvin Kahn of Highlands County, Moses Jumper, the former Director of the Seminole Recreation Department, got together with the Bowers deciding to initiate a special event to commemorate Junior Cypress, the past Foreman of the Big Cypress Cattle Program. Former Tribal Chairman Mitchell Cypress says that "when I think of my uncle, I see him on the back of a horse with his hat pulled down, sheltering his eyes from the sun or driving around the Rez with a pickup truck load of kids heading to the cow pens or swimming hole."

The Seminole Tribe dates back to the early 1600's and today is one of the leading cattle businesses in the state. The Tribe strives to preserve their unique history and culture, expanding their enterprises into economic success. Thousands of visitors from all over the world visit the Reservation and enjoy many events in the modern entertainment complex. One of the most beautiful exhibits depicting the history of the Seminoles is the life-like scenes housed in the Ah-Tah-Thi-Ki Museum which opened in 1997. Visitors are also invited to stroll down long shaded boardwalks learn from informative signs details about Florida's native trees.

The Junior Cypress Cracker Trail and Rodeo offers an adventure for all visitors and acknowledges an appreciation for the Big Cypress Indian Tribe that supports its youth and preserves its history.

The Junior Cypress Entertainment Complex is surrounded by thousands of acres of unspoiled land preserved by the Tribe. The complex and arena names is named in honor of Junior Cypress, the 30 year past foreman for the Big Cypress Cattle Program who worked as a "cowhand for local ranchers".

The Big Cypress Reservation information states that "cattle" is their first Tribal industry but are expanded in many other directions while preserving their independent and prosperous in the highly competitive world of the 21st Century.

FOUR

"THE APIARIST"

THE ANCIENT ART OF BEEKEEPING

RENE CURTIS PRATT

HAROLD P. CURTIS HONEY STORE

LABELLE

Dating back to the Egyptians some 5,000 years ago, humans have been keeping bees. In those early days, humans observed wild bees flying from flower-to-flower depositing a yellow substance (pollen) and soon noticed that the flower ripened into fruits or vegetables. Not only did early humans witness "pollination" but also succumbed to the sweet taste of bee nectar.

Beekeepers known as "Apiarists," domesticated wild hives for honey production and began to create other marketable by-products from the industrious bees. One of these unique by-products is "propolis" (bee glue made from tree resin to seal open spaces in the hive and used in ancient times to heal wounds). Other by-products are beeswax (secreted by Worker Bees onto scales of their abdomen later discarded in the hive) and Royal Jelly (a substance secreted by Worker Bees fed to the larvae of a potential Queen Bee). The beekeeper or "Apiarist" is the human caretaker of the hive's production.

Harold P. Curtis and his family are fourth generation Apiarists in Labelle, Florida, opening the honey store in 1921.

Today, his son and daughter, Rene Curtis Pratt and James Curtis run the store. It has "blossomed" into one of the most popular tourist attractions and health centered businesses in Central Florida with a worldwide reputation. For the past seventy years, located in the heart of LaBelle's historic district, 335 Bridge Street, walking distance to the beautiful Caloosahatchee River, the Curtis family has been hand-bottling pure honey in the store's back room and selling it. Above one of the shelves, magnifying the family's long history is a framed picture of founder Harold B. Curtis who today spends most of his time producing and saving the endangered Queen Bee. "Several years ago, the Queen Bee's life expectancy was 3 to 4 years; today it is 1 year," says Rene. "Polluting by-products of Florida's explosive population growth is threatening bee colonies. There is only one fertile Queen Bee in a beehive and, today, the approximate 3 million hives in the State are in jeopardy."

Florida bee colonies are negatively affected by widespread radiation from cell phone towers, (disturbing the life cycle of the bee's reproduction system and honey production), environmental/chemical and Agra-pollution. Besides these human created concerns, "another threat to the hive is the invasive beetle and mite, such as the Varro Intestinal Mite that sneaks into vulnerable hives by attaching to the bee like a flea on a dog, then feasts on the colony's young brood," Rene explains. "These insects also introduce pesticides and fungal pathogens into the hive that can collapse the entire colony."

"A little-known fact about bees" explains Rene is that "by their

Nature, they like dark skies; however, with developments sprawling throughout Florida and the introduction of bright artificial lights, bees swarm to the light distracting them from returning to the hive to do their work."

"There is also the threat of Africanized bees," says Rene. "Since 1965, we have had to breed, or buy, our own Queens since most hives have been infiltrated. They have a different DNA and fly away from the hive. Now my dad is raising our own Queens. We cross-breed our Queens to keep them producing. This is how we propagate the hive colony."

Rene is a very talented "Apiarist" and treats the bees like "family;" even her grandchildren "talk" to the bees. "One time, one of my grandsons lifted open one of the bee boxes but the bees ignored him and kept right on with their honey-making business. "Bees react to 'fear.' It is only the male bee that stings. I have been stung only once or twice over the many years I have been collecting beeswax and honey from the hive as bees learn a caretaker's deposition. Unlike the wasp, a bee dies after it empties its entire body into the sting."

"Working with bees is an intricate process but very rewarding," adds Rene. "Honey made by bees is pure and provides healing properties.

We also use their beeswax to make non-drip candles that we sell in the store; they are the cleanest and most fragrant candles you can buy," Rene emphasizes. "The candles purify the air and eliminate bad odors. We also make soap, and sell homemade jellies made by a friend of mine."

Rene is an expert on bee behavior. "Bees work by the season when flowers bloom as they fly from flower-to-flower propagating them with the needed pollen they collect. The process of pollination begins with the female bee flying from male to female flowers of various crops. The female workers keep the hive functioning while male bees mostly just eat and fertilize the Queen."

In the Spring, when orange trees are blooming, Rene sets out the bee hive boxes in citrus groves to produce Orange Blossom honey then takes them to Sanibel Island to produce Seagrape and Mangrove honey; they also bottle Palmetto and Wildflower honey. Bees fly in a radius of about two miles from their hive and are going to many kinds of flowering plants. It takes two to eight weeks to make honey and to be ready for bottling. Honey contains about 60 calories per tablespoon.

"Bees have a sophisticated, yet simplistic behavior to gather nectar from flowers. The Worker bee puts out its 'tongue' or 'straw' into the flower to collect nectar and pollen to make honey to feed the hive. As they chew the honey and mix it with their saliva, it forms 'Beeswax' which they spit out to build Honeycomb, a six-sided cell filled and covered with wax where they store nectar and protect their young. Worker bees have 8 pairs of wax glands under their abdomen and produce a small amount of wax on their scales. Worker bees have baskets on their legs to gather the pollen and 'set' the fruits or vegetables.' The Worker bee scrapes off the wax from the scales or pollen baskets using their spines. The nectar is put into the honeycomb cells and is capped with wax to seal it."

Making honey from the hives is a sophisticated removal process. "The beehive consists of two layers in the bee box with a screen. At the top of the box is pollen and honey, nectar is on the bottom. The screen is taken out and we stand it up in our 'Uncapper' machine in the back of the store.

The Uncapper spins for twenty minutes to separate the wax and honeycomb. We then take the cleaned rack out and place it back into the hive.

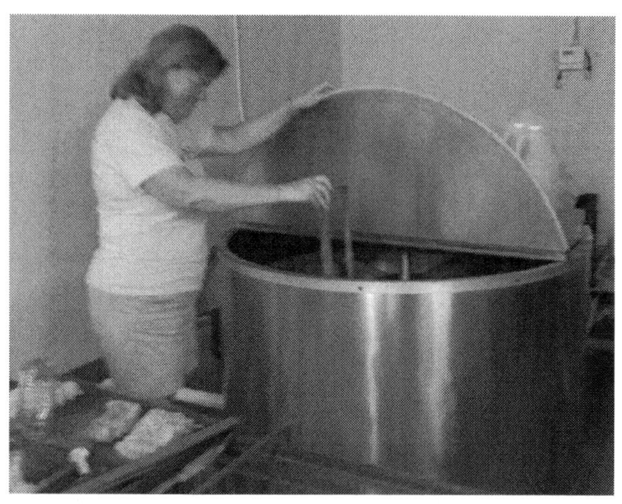

The honey now settles for 24 hours in a 'holding tank' until it is ready to be piped into several drums with different types of honey.

We sit at the end of the drums and bottle the honey by hand. It then is ready to be labeled and put on the shelves for sale."

"We collect honey several times a week and bottle our own raw, unfiltered honey to preserve the quality of the pollen. One of the most frequently asked questions to us by visitors: 'Is our honey raw and unprocessed?' Yes, it is! Our honey is not cooked or processed. Honey that is overheated beyond 180 degrees is imported from China and does not have healing properties. One of the outstanding qualities of honey is its healing properties. If you are coming down with a cold, eat honey, as it boosts the immune system. Some beekeepers use the bee 'sting' to heal certain health conditions that is the ancient science of 'Apitherapy,' Rene explains.

An article in Holistic Medicine (2016) says bee venom attacks inflammation. The stinger has been used to treat Fibromyalgia, Multiple Sclerosis, Arthritis and other human ailments. Some European doctors use the bee venom to make a serum. According to Fred Finkelman, University of Cincinnati College of Medicine, "Understanding the evolution of allergic responses is a new beginning, more than the end of a story."

Rene explains how the bee stinging process works. A long tweezer is used to place the bee on the skin. The stinger is left inside the person to 'pulsate' and empty its venom. When the stinger quits pulsating, it is empty and can be scratched out. However, for everyday treatment of bee stings, you can apply baking soda, vinegar, or meat tenderizer to take away pain. If I am stung, I do nothing!"

Another little-known fact about bees is that they use electromagnetic energy. Since the 1960's, scientists have been aware of the "electric" side of pollination. Botanists suggest that electric forces enhance the attraction of bees to certain flowers for pollination. Professor Robert Clarke, Physicist, University of Bristol, says "Bumble bees can sense the electric field surrounding a flower and can determine the sweetness of the bloom by their shape. This is another very new field of study."

How do you story honey? It does not need refrigeration but if it becomes condensed over time, Rene suggests "simply put the bottle in the sun or heat it in a small pan of water to return it to its liquid consistency. We also use pollen to make Royal Jelly (the Queen's only diet) and 'Propolis' eaten to neutralize bacteria, fungi and viruses. Matter of fact, bee pollen is said to be the perfect food! We also sell a unique product called 'Bee Caps' a company founded by Tony Hueston, Sr. who writes the following story:

"In 1986, my mother, Pauline 'Grandma' Hueston was hospitalized in critical condition suffering from 8 separate very serious medical problems. She eventually had to have bypass surgery. We thought she might die. A friend from Europe sent four bottles of bee pollen, royal jelly, Propolis and raw honey to Grandma. She was told it would improve her appetite and regain her strength. After 3 months, she became strong, increased her stamina and strength. She lived to nearly 90 years old enjoying her family."

"If a beginner wants to start a beehive, the first step is to purchase an established hive," Rene explains. "The hive consists of one Queen, or Mother Bee, that lays some 50,000 eggs fertilized by the male Drones. The eggs hatch in twenty-one days to produce a "Worker" or female bee and twenty-four days to produce a 'Drone' or male."

The industrious production of honey is the bee's life work, and then it dies. It is said that bees work themselves to death. Thus, this story is a tribute to the life of Bees, their contribution to human health, natural crop production, and to their enduring Caretakers, the Apiarists.

FIVE

THE BIRTH OF SYMBIOTIC ORGANIC AGRICULTURE WAYMORE FARMS

BRYAN BEER II, OWNER
CLEWISTON

Quietly tucked away in bountiful scrub country, 11 miles east of LaBelle, the "call of the wild" is rejuvenated at the Waymore Farms in Clewiston.

"We want to leave a positive imprint on everything we touch," says Bryan Beer, 35, owner of the unique Waymore Farms in

Clewiston. The turkeys, chickens, beef, ducks, hogs, and the land are a living reflection of Beer's conviction set into motion with animals grazing on organic forage as part of his Master Plan to treat both animals and the land with respect.

Beer is "living his passion" that started as a youngster growing up in a 5th generation family of citrus growers then later earning a BA degree in Agricultural Science from Purdue University. He was inspired to create Waymore Farms because he "wanted to do something other than conventional agriculture." In 2009, Beer watched a TV documentary by Joel Salatin of Polyface Farm, a 3rd generation alternative farming family in Virginia's Shenandoah Valley, about "symbiotic agriculture." Beer liked the concept and began researching the possibility of replicating a symbiotic organic farm on his land in Clewiston, Florida.

Symbiotic agriculture," says Beer "is a new concept with a goal of increasing production of organic poultry, hogs, cows, and eggs with each stage complementing the next utilizing the natural environment."

Waymore Farms is now in its third year of organic production with Beer managing and fine tuning the care of the land, animals, and marketing the end product of organic meats/eggs to fine dining restaurants, family dinner tables and Farmer's Markets across the state with the heartbeat of the operation in Clewiston.

At Waymore Farms, the first stage of production begins with a flock ranging anywhere from 300 to 1000 chicks housed in a large pin or "brooder" until maturity when they are transferred to a mobile 10 x 12 x 3 foot "tractor unit" that is rotated every 24 hours over the 300 acres of pasture, capturing natural fertilizer in the soil and conditioning the land.

"When the chickens are about 6 weeks old or three to 4 pounds, we process them on site. The land is now ready for the next stage of symbiotic farming: Foraging cattle."

Raising cows for organic beef, Beer bred his commercial herd to a Red Devon sire that he says, "finishes on grass like Angus on grain, as a cow's rumen is adapted to digesting grass; we never feed grain as a supplement and do not feed the cows any hormones or antibiotics. If we purchase an additional cow for the herd, it has to be free of antibiotics or it is culled."

At Waymore Farms, to achieve the highest production of organic cattle, Beer incorporates a symbiotic farming methodology termed "mob grazing." "Mob grazing provides the highest and best use of the land, placing as many cows as sustainable per acre. When cows are weaned at about 7 months, they are put out to pasture until a slaughter weight is achieved between 1100 or 1250 pounds," explains Beer. Individual Chefs like Matt Germain at the Quart House Restaurant (LaBelle), Naples and other high-end restaurants across the state have specific weight requirements to purchase organic beef. "I have been working 6 or 7 years to master this concept and by 2017 we project we will be incorporating rabbit and lamb into our production, as well as continuing to market organic pasteurized hogs, duck, and chicken eggs."

Chefs Jeff and Jessica Acol of "A Table Apart" Restaurant in Bonita Springs purchase their organic chickens from Waymore Farms. Chef Jessica says, the "Waymore chicken is a delicious product done with quality and integrity. Bryan Beer, the owner, provides a quality. Our job at A Table Apart is to bring that quality to the diners of southwest Florida." One of their featured dishes is "**Poulet Basquaise**".

The recipe:

INGREDIENTS:

1 whole Waymore Farms Chicken Cut into stewing pieces
1/2 onion julienned
2 red bell pepper julienned
2 green bell pepper julienned
1 teaspoon epaulette pepper
2 cups chicken broth/stock
1/2 cup white wine
1 large tomato medium dice
1 teaspoon fresh thyme
2 tablespoon olive oil
3 cloves of garlic sliced
Salt and pepper

Season the chicken with the salt and pepper. Reheat pan on medium heat with the olive oil.
Sear chicken until each side is brown. Once browned remove chicken and set on side.
Add onions, bell pepper, garlic and sauté until soft.
Add tomato, thyme and epaulette pepper, sauté for a minute.
Deglaze with white wine then pour in the chicken stock.
Add browned chicken back to the pan cover and braise for 45 minutes on medium heat.
Check seasoning at end of cooking adding more salt, pepper or epaulette to taste.

"I have lived my whole life with a profound love of the ocean and land. I grew up in Hawaii. At "A Table Apart", we have decided to take a step in the right direction and focus on sustainable seafood and natural meats," says Chef Jeff.

Another restaurant that purchases Waymore Farm products is Chef Mike Mueller, owner of Café Lurcart Naples. The restaurant serves "American Comfort Cuisine." Chef Mueller says, "As a child he spent his whole life cooking and even dressed like a Chef." He says he likes the intensity, energy, and artistic flare as a Chef creating new dishes." He received his training in New York City and collaborated with his Godfather who owns the restaurant to bring his creative dishes to the public.

One of his favorite recipes is **Crispy Pollo Loco with Achiote-Chili Rub and Avocado Crema.**

Ingredients:

1 ea Semi boneless chicken

Paste

3.5 oz Achiote
1/3 Cup Chicken Stock

Rocoto Rub

1 Tbl creamed roasted garlic
2 tsp salt
1 Tbl Achiote Paste
2 Tbl Rocoto Paste
2 tsp aji amarillo liquid
1 Tbl Parsley rough Chop
2 tsp garlic oil

Grn Chimichrurri

1 Chopped Parsley
1 Chopped Oregano
1 Roasted Garlic slivers
1 Julliene aji amarillo

1 Roasted Garlic Oil
.5 C Lime juice
Salt

Avocado-Chili Crema

48 ea Serrano .5 seeded
16 C Cilantro
32 Garlic confit
4 Sour Cream
1 Lime Juice
2 Tbl Salt and Black Pepper
8 ea Avocado Diced
*Blend everything but avocado until smooth. Add avocado and blend smooth.
5 ea Halved tomato and one roasted spring onion

Methodology:

1. Simmer stock and Achiote and whisk together
2. Blend all ingredients for the rub and reserve.
3. Add 1.5 Tbl and Rub under skin

Lurcrat's distinctive flavors are complemented with a global list of 200 wines. Café Lurcat's chef driven menu features sophisticated American cuisine prepared from fresh seasonal ingredients. The restaurant was voted by Food and Wine Magazine as having the "10 Best Wine Lists."

Waymore Farms is popular among chefs because Beer is always introducing and expanding his selection of products. "We are also doing turkeys for the first time this year for Thanksgiving. We only have a limited number so we are requiring people to preorder them with a deposit. The cost of the turkeys will be $7/lb.; they are 100% pasture raised and 100% organic. We received some outstanding feedback from our trial turkeys, so we are really excited about that. We also expanded our duck and chicken egg operation quite substantially. We will be having around 70 dozen chicken eggs, and 25 dozen duck eggs per day," says Beer.

"On Waymore Farms, we also have what we call a 'Waymore Hog,' a cross between a wild and domestic gene. Domestic hogs are bigger and have more 'muscle mass;' the wild gene has more flavor. We breed some hogs at 8 months old. Our pastured pork is rotated across the pastures and through the woods, producing a healthy hog in a natural environment. Part of the day, we release hogs into a cooling pond where they cluster, splash and swim as they do in the wild and have the space to roam freely. This year, 2016, will be out first hog production. We process them at a slaughter house when they reach 200-260 pounds."

At every stage of symbiotic organic farming on Waymore Farms,

Beer strives to eliminate a stressful environment and overcrowded conditions to produce better meat. Two donkeys also add to the entourage roaming freely over the property warding off coyotes, raccoons, possums and other potential predators.

As the sun begins to fade into dusk and sinks below the horizon, the long day for Beer doesn't end. He makes sure all the animals are bedded down securely before he retires. After spending most of his daylight hours outside, gathering cows, working the land composting the pastures and citrus trees, the quiet night brings a time for reflection as he looks over his flock with satisfaction, the product of hard work, determination, and perseverance. With Beer's passion and respect for the land and the animals, Waymore Farms is a living example of nurturing life and evolving the food chain into healthy organics. He dedicates himself to educating the public through talks and tours "down on the farm" with a friendly Charolais cow who invites visitors to pet him.

As creeping urbanization in Florida gradually distances humans from the land, Waymore Farm's mission is to cultivate organic farming, bring healthy food to the dinner table and educate visitors about "symbiotic agriculture." As Bryan Beer packs in for the night, he shakes hands with Nature and acknowledges: "This is my life."

SIX

CITY OF OAKS

LABELLE

The Heart of old Florida is revived beneath the ancient shady oaks in the "City of Oaks," LaBelle, Florida.

Traveling a short jog off U.S. 27 north onto State Road 29 West, it's like gradually lifting a shadowed veil of history and rediscovering the roots of over 200 years of Florida's cultural heritage. This short travel distance back in time re-lives the story of the pioneer spirit preserved in the beautiful town of LaBelle, Florida, population 4,588 (2013).

The community leaders of LaBelle have refurbished many old structures that give new life to the "way it was" in the 1800s such as the building that houses the LaBelle Heritage Museum. The Museum maintains a large collection of local artifacts and documents reflecting an appreciation of the traditional lifestyle of early settlers. Traveling further west on State Road 29 through downtown, LaBelle borders the natural beauty of the Caloosahatchee River where visitors can walk, canoe, kayak by day or under the dark night skies displaying a blanket of stars where the only sound heard is "silence."

Old traditions live in LaBelle through natural preserves such as Barron Park on the River by the bridge and other planned preserves postured on the edge of the Lake Wales Ridge that runs more than 200 miles through the spine of Florida.

After the last Ice Age, more than 11,000 years ago, Hendry County sported an ancient beach when the sea level fluctuated and the Florida peninsula arose from the bottom of the sea.

Closer to the present time, in the 1800's after three Seminole Indian Wars, new pioneer "cow hunters" began to settle in Central Florida. The "adventurers" gathered their cow herds, packed up their families in covered wagons and headed south through rugged Wild Florida. As cattle rancher Dewey Fusell, whose family settled in the Green Swamp (Polk County) remembers, "my great, granddaddy told me "little baby Lewis had to learn to walk all over again when he climbed out of the wagon through nothing but swamp and high water."

LaBelle is old Florida at its best. Visitors can experience those early days in the successful shops of family businesses that line State Road 29, such as the Harold P. Curtis Honey House, who started the family business in 1945, one of the first in the town. Down the street there are more shops of interest. The old antique shop is an inviting place where visitors can browse for lost treasures to add to their own environment, dine across the street at the famed Flora and Ella's Restaurant or walk around the corner to the Bridge Street Coffee and Tea House for an after-dinner delight.

Traveling further west, St. Rd. 29 dead ends into the historic Hendry County Court House built in 1926 in the Mediterranean-Revival style by Edward Hosful where justice is still today reckoned and laws enforced, unlike the old days of Wild Florida and Bone Mizell in the turbulent days of the 1800's range wars when justice was meted out by the toughest "cow hunter" protecting his family, herd, and property from cattle rustlers. (In the 1800's, cattle ranchers were called "cow hunters" as they had to gather up their cows for long cattle drives to coastal markets by pulling them out of swamps, palmettos, and shrubs).

Today one of the biggest and most successful events in LaBelle is the Swamp Cabbage Festival celebrating its 50th year in February. The event attracts visitors the world over. There are vendors making swamp cabbage, other foods, and the excitement of the traditional armadillo races. The festival also offers an opportunity to take a rustic boat cruise down the Caloosahatchee River. It is a huge celebration!

LaBelle is a unique community established by Captain Francis A.

Hendry when in 1889 the new settlement became “LaBelle" by combining the two first names of Hendry’s sisters into the name of the community.” Many families in LaBelle, who set down roots in the once rugged land, stayed for many generations and today grew the community into a thriving lifestyle and land based economy of cattle and agriculture.

As cattle ranching is still prime in Hendry County, one long time business, LaBelle Ranch Supply owned by father and son, Brad and Rodney Murray, stock boots, saddles, feed, animal medicine, rifles and handguns, “cow hunter” books along with a display of cowboy hats along the walls collected from local pioneer “cow hunters.” Brad Murray, graduate of LaBelle High School and Embry Riddle, whose scholarship fostered his plunge into Professional Baseball as a Pitcher with the Chicago White Socks, eventually came back home to LaBelle and with his dad and bought the present store.

For entertainment, food, and family fun, one of the most unique new restaurants, The Quart House, recently opened at the old location of the famous Long Branch Saloon, offering a lengthy choice of selections for lunch and dinner serving beer, wine, green tea, other beverages and providing a unique dining experience. Bryan Beer and Executive Chef, Matt Germain teamed-up in 1965 to pursue a joint venture and become restaurant proprietors.

What is unique about the Quart House food is Chef Germain's wide variety of organic dishes he created made with locally grown vegetables served in a variety of tasty dishes.

One of the specialty offerings on the large raw food salad bar are the delicious "cucamelons," a small cucumber. There is also organic bok choy, duck eggs, beets and a special Protein Platter with burger or grilled chicken breast, Brussel sprouts and locally grown collard greens, topped with a fried egg. The Chef also creates other traditional dishes such as Angus steak, blackened chicken salad, "Angry shrimp" and a classic Quart House burger with a selection of toppings.

Visitors can eat inside or out on the large front terrace and order take-out at the drive-through window. Friday's locals gather in the fresh air on the terrace to socialize and enjoy the musical entertainment of Randy Cormier from 6:30-9:30 p.m. along with an offering of Sushi rolls. The Quart House is open 6 days a week, 11-9 Monday-Sat. and Sunday, 10-3 p.m. Phone: 674-7141

The LaBelle community is a small town, stretching to grow into the future supporting local businesses, educational opportunities at Florida Southwestern State College, sports, good food and fun. As Mayor Lyons says, "LaBelle has many small businesses in the LaBelle Chamber of Commerce and we invite everyone to discover Old Florida here where the beautiful Caloosahatchee

River meets Old Florida under the oaks. I am fortunate and blessed to live in LaBelle."

SEVEN

THE BEAUTIFUL AND INTELLIGENT FLORIDA NATIVE BLACK BEAR

MIKE ORLANDO
ASSISTANT COORDINATOR, BEAR MANAGEMENT PROGRAM
FLORIDA FISH AND WILDLIFE CONSERVATION COMMISSION
WEKIWA SPRINGS STATE PARK
APOPKA

Since 1980, Florida's native black bear population has been expanding, estimated, by Florida Fish and Wildlife to number approximately 4,350. The same year, the human population in

Florida numbered 5 million; in 2016, the population grew to 20 million with an expected growth by 2060 to 36 million people. Today, bears and people are living in close proximity but Florida's black bears still live in the sand pine wilderness, forests, oak scrub, and wetlands, adapting to the encroachment of humans into their native habitat. It is not the bears that pose the greatest threat to their survival; it is human behavior.

After the last Ice Age, eleven thousand years ago, Paleo-Indians occupied much of Florida. Their descendants, the tattooed Timucua Indians, fished and hunted along the upward flowing St. John's River on Florida's northeast coast and inland to the Wekiwa River. Today, one of the most beautiful bear habitats in Florida is Wekiwa Springs State Park, Apopka, FL, about 20 miles north of Orlando and the origin of a spring that pumps 42 million gallons of water a day into the Wekiwa River from a deep 15 to 20-foot cavern. The Wekiwa Springs River runs through Wekiwa Springs State Park and is one of the last remaining wild and scenic rivers in Florida.

Today, Wekiwa Springs State Park, originally a private Sportsman's Club in 1941, is a large tourist attraction with camping, swimming, canoeing, biking, hiking and horseback riding through the 100-year-old pine forest flats. As the sun rises and dusk veils the forest, visitors can observe white tail deer, wild turkeys, the little-known Sherman's fox squirrel and the dark profile of Florida's black bear peacefully roaming through the woods.

Mike Orlando, Assistant Coordinator of the Bear Management Program, Florida Fish and Wildlife Conservation Commission says, "The Park is one of the best protected habitats for the black bear to safely survive." He dispels the widely-held belief that the growing human population in Florida imperils the black bear, as he says, "they have recovered. It is not true that as the population grows, natural species necessarily decrease. Today, better education of tourists, residents and good management practices like habitat management has helped the black bear and other wildlife thrive.

For the past twenty years, Orlando has studied the behavior of the Florida black bear, one of the most curious and wondrous species in Florida. He says, "The male bears have a territorial area of sixty square miles and females, a smaller range of fifteen square miles."

At Wekiwa Springs State Park, a housing development butts directly up to the edge. Orlando calls this a "transitional zone or urban wildlife interface." People who live in the residential community are educated to co-exist with their bear neighbors. However, Orlando brings up a caveat: "Bears have a keen sense of smell, so residents not only living directly on the park border but the neighborhood need to follow safety procedures to divert an opportunistic bear hunting for food. It is important to move any eminent food from the area. In order to save the bear, humans need to be careful not to create life conflicts. If a bear approaches a neighborhood, it is likely seeking available unsecured human food," Orlando clarifies.

"In January or February," says Orlando, "Female bears, about 3 years old, usually bare their young. They may pull together pine needles or fallen trees, whatever is around to build a den like a bird's nest, and some even dig a hole. Females usually have 2 or 3 cubs. The females protect the cubs, teach them how to survive and find food. If the mother bear learns there is food available in a neighborhood, she will also teach her cubs where to find it." FWC literature says if a bear is eating something on your property, take note of what it is and secure it after the bear has left the area. In Florida, it is against the law to feed bears.

The Florida Fish and Wildlife Conservation Commission (FWC) has developed a "cost share program" to help residents afford bear resistant containers. Residents can purchase "bear proof dumpsters" for their area like the ones at Wekiwa Springs State

Park. Highlands Hammock State Park in Sebring has numerous bear sightings and is also installing the new dumpsters. However, despite the closer proximity of bears and humans, Orlando says, "Bears usually withdraw from an accidental confrontation with humans; however, they are wild animals and deserve respect.

"The best precaution to co-exist in a bear habitat," says Orlando "is to keep attractants away from bears. If a bear is up a tree, usually after dark, it will eventually leave the area on its own when it feels safe. People sometimes mistake bear 'posturing' like standing up on its hind legs as a threat," he explains. "The bear behaves like a squirrel. When a bear stands on its hind legs, it is only trying to get a better view or scent. However, unlike squirrels, bears are powerful. Males can weigh on an average 250-350 pounds; females, 130-180 pounds. Because of their power and size, people should respect these animals and stay at a safe distance.

Orlando stresses that "pro-active" human behavior is essential to protect bears and all native wildlife. As people continue to migrate into the sunshine state, bear and people encounters in the woods or in neighborhoods will continue; however, Orlando emphasizes, "People can learn to co-exist with Nature and appreciate the bear."

"Bears are symbols of the wilderness. We provide information and teach our visitors about bear behavior, we go to schools and take a bear hide from one accidentally killed on the highway to show children. We hand out bear whistles and clappers to kids and adults to scare a bear away should there be an encounter. Most importantly, if we appreciate the natural world and realize we are inherently connected with Nature, we as humans will learn to appreciate the life of wild things in preserving Florida's wildlife. We are a living planet and we need to teach a balance of human behavior with Nature exploration. We have to do our part to save the bear."

In 2016, FWC provided Florida residents the opportunity for input on the next planned bear hunt. The Commission was presented with four options to consider as recommended by staff at FWC and biologists. Each option outlined a different strategy. Option 1, was "the same as the 2015 framework with updated hunt objectives;" Option 2 offered more "limited restrictions on hunting bears;" Option 3 offered "a postponement of bear hunting in 2016, creating a zero-hunt objective;" Option 4, opted "to repeal bear hunt rules and not allow bear hunting in Florida in future years." The result was no bear hunting for 2016.

Mike Orlando has been studying bears since college. He earned his BA degree in Wildlife Ecology from the University of Florida and later his Master's in "Forest Ecology" at the University of Kentucky. At UF his study of alligators migrated to a bear project at Eglin Air Force Base when he worked with graduate students placing radio collars on bears. At Weeki Wachee Springs on Florida's Gulf Coast, Orlando expanded his focus on bear behavior which led him to his present position as the FWC Assistant Coordinator of the Bear Management Program.

(Thank you to Brenda Broder, Ranger, Highlands Hammock State Park for her assistance in this story)

EIGHT
FORT FRASER TRAIL

GUEST CONTRIBUTOR: JENNIFER SWAIN, EDITOR

LAKELAND

"On Sept. 28, 1850, after Florida became a state in 1845, an Act of Congress gave all swamp and overflowed lands belonging to the United States to Florida. The land was donated to the State for the purpose of being reclaimed. The Estimated lands were twelve million acres."

Population of Florida in 1865: 464,639. (Book by G. R. Fairbanks, published 1808)

Traveling north to Lakeland on U.S. 98 through Central Florida, the semi-rustic 7.7-mile Fort Fraser bike trail/pedestrian path parallels the highway, winding its way by warehouses and business developments, carved into the miles of hundred-year-old trees that preserve the natural beauty of the land.

Along the trail is an engraved sign memorializing Fort Fraser, one of many Florida forts established to protect New World Europeans colonizing Florida. In 1838, Colonel Zachary Taylor was Commander of the 1st U.S. Infantry stationed at Fort Fraser. Due to the influx of new world explorers, Andrew Jackson urged Congress to pass the 'Indian Removal Act"' forcing Native Americans mostly the Cherokee Nation who occupied much of the land, to move to government set-aside "Reservations."

Confirmed by Treaty of Mouthier, the process began. The three Seminole Indian Wars resulted, leader Osceola and others were arrested and confined. Some twenty thousand Indians were marched 2,200 miles at gun point with no belongings to western Reservations. In freezing temperatures, Native people were loaded onto wagons or on horseback to travel the grueling route that came to be known as the "Trail of Tears."

Today, Florida's population is expected to triple throughout the 21st Century attracting people to re-locate into the Sunshine State. Concrete housing developments are rapidly growing, encroaching upon the pristine land of Central Florida with little restriction, due to vast monetary gains. How will this 21st Century challenge be addressed to preserve and protect the last of the pristine wilderness?

NINE
"MAN OF MANY TALENTS"
BROWN "BROWNIE" AKERS
FLORIDA STATE PARK RANGER

STEPHEN FOSTER STATE PARK
SUWANNEE RIVER

Brown "Brownie" Akers is a multi-talented "one of kind" man. He is a man of Nature who has traveled the United States as a singer/songwriter, plays the mandolin and today, works as a Florida State Park Ranger at Stephen Foster State Park, a career he began at age 59.

In September 2014, Akers followed the "call of the wild" that eventually led him to Stephen Foster State Park where he began as a volunteer at one of the most famous parks in the United States. His mentor was, and still is, Stephanie McClain, Assistant Park Manager.

The Park nestled along the banks of 246 miles, wild black water, Suwannee River in White Springs, Florida rose from the Okefenokee Swamp in Georgia which flows southward into Florida and has been inhabited for thousands of years. The Timacua Indians, who poled down the upward flowing St. John's River on Florida's east coast, occupied the "suwani" or Echo River, rich in sulfur. In the 20th Century, White Springs flourished for many years as a popular health resort attracting famous visitors such as Teddy Roosevelt and Hendry Ford who came to experience the healing waters. What remains of the once famous health spa is the concrete wall and gate now near the entrance of Stephen Foster

State Park.

Stephen Foster State Park opened in 1950 when the Stephen Foster Memorial Commission developed the park as a tribute to the songwriter who gave birth to the State song: "Way Down Upon the Suwannee River." Then in 1953, the park initiated the first traditional Florida Folk Festival celebrated annually every Memorial Day Weekend.

Although famous composer Stephen Foster never visited Florida, many of his songs express and preserve the southern American Minstrel in ballads such as "Old Folks at Home", "My Old Kentucky Home" and "Beautiful Dreamer." Called the 'Father of Music', Stephen Foster was born on the 4th of July 1826.

Paralleling the life of Stephen Foster who had a reputation as a creative thinker who followed his own destiny, Brownie Akers travels a similar path. Foster was a self-taught musician, had only a brief formal education in Pennsylvania, joined a Minstrel Band and wrote songs. Foster and Akers lives both reflect an image larger than life through their work.

As an explorer, Akers found his way to Florida from Knoxville, Tennessee, his hometown, by way of Montana. Akers's mom and dad owned a company in Montana that built rawhide saddle trees. Saddle trees are designed to fit the horse, balance the rider and make the saddle sturdier. Akers says his "real world education began after he graduated from Knoxville High School." "I joined the family business selling horse packing equipment and technologically advanced products for the saddle industry getting my education as a salesman."

"In Montana, my grandfather owned a rambling thirty-one-acre farm near Bozeman. The centerpiece of the property was a 1914 estate home surrounded by manicured gardens. My two older brothers and I helped on the estate where I spent a lot of time learning how to do physical jobs. When my grandfather passed way in 1992, the family sold the property and I decided to move on. I bought a travel trailer and began to explore the United States working as an independent contractor. I maintained yards, pools and took any job I could find. This was a great experience as I got paid to workout. I lived a life of labor," says Akers which is reflected in his fitness today.

Akers constant companion on his travels was his music. "I learned to play the mandolin, an 8-string instrument originating in Italy. The mandolin is smaller than the guitar and there are many styles and types," adding, "it was the mandolin that picked me at the age of 50. I am self-taught."

As Akers followed his dreams to Florida, he started working as a volunteer at St. Joseph Peninsular State Park on the Gulf of Mexico alongside a 9.5-mile snowy white beach. He lived at the park for four months then returned to Montana in the Spring. In 2014, the direction of his magical life says Akers, "fell from the sky." It was through the words of a yardman who suggested to

Akers that "I volunteer at Stephen Foster Sate Park in White Springs." On September 3, 2015, after serving his apprenticeship as a new volunteer at Stephen Foster State Park, he was hired as a Resident Ranger.

Today, Akers shares his musical talent with thousands of visitors to Stephen Foster State Park providing entertainment at camper programs and other park events. "I put together the Shaffer Hill Rock and Roll Blues Band. We play music like Bobby Blue Bland, B.B. King, Howling Wolf, Etta James and the King of Blues, Bill Monroe. When I write music it also just falls out of the sky."

"The rewards of a Park Ranger are not monetary but aesthetic," Akers says, "preserving Florida's wilderness with the self-satisfaction of providing meaningful experiences for park visitors. The wisdom I have attained as a Ranger has given me a new awareness of the biodiversity in Florida and the biomass index of animal and plant life. Life here thrives and is productive; I watch it every day. As Park Rangers, we promote and persevere to support restoring Nature and the natural resources. However, there is a caveat: With the increased population influx into Florida, we are confronted with a battle to preserve the wilderness. The main culprit is creeping urbanization and the loss of biomass or habit. We need to preserve habitat to support wildlife such as the endangered scrub blue jays and other species. I cannot promote urbanization. Although some animals can live in an urban environment, many animals starve. Some visitors think of Florida only as white beaches, condos, golf courses with every inch developed. People will spend $30 or $40 a day at Disneyworld while the native habitat along I-4 suffers, i.e. the birds, bears and alligators. Another caveat of the growth of human population in wilderness areas is that some of the wild species become used to humans and are not scared to come in closer proximity, thus, threatening the existence of wildlife. The most valuable contribution of Florida's State Parks and Rangers is to protect and preserve the Wild. Our mission also is to raise peoples' awareness of the opportunity to become part of the solution as a Park Ranger. Anyone, at any age, can become a park volunteer. The American

Corp is a volunteer organization where kids can be mentored as young Rangers and receive pay."

Akers greets hundreds of visitors to Stephen Foster State Park, talks with them, guides them through the park, helps them build campfires and contributes to an unforgettable experience. Sleeping under a canopy of stars at the close of the day is a rare opportunity that Akers has the privilege of doing every night. Time spent at Stephen Foster State Park is truly filled with nonexpendable moments when time slows down and peace envelops the world.

The man and the career that chose Brownie Akers, offers visitors to Stephen Foster State Park knowledge, experience and insight into Nature for all those who meet him. His personality and character are immersed in a lifestyle connected to the land and his gift is an appreciation of life that awakens and renews the human spirit.

TEN

"IT IS NOT JUST THE BIRDS WHO ARE RUNNING OUT OF WATER BUT PEOPLE TOO"

Crested caracara (threatened)

GUEST CONTRIBUTOR: *PAUL GRAY, Ph.D. SCIENCE COORDINATOR*

EVERGLADES RESTORATION PROGRAM

AUDUBON SOCIETY

Florida is world famous for its birds. Our location and geography create variety, including tropical and oceanic species not seen in other parts of the US, unique resident subspecies, migrants coming and going from all over the Americas, and lots and lots of large showy birds. Pelicans, flamingoes, spoonbills, frigates, anhingas, storks, cranes, herons, egrets, ibis, limpkins, kites, caracaras, boobies, tropicbirds…the list of exotic and dramatic birds goes on and on. Of the approximately 800 species of birds found in North America, about half can be found in Florida.

Wood storks (endangered) and black necked stilts

Most people have heard of the immense wading bird nesting colonies that astonished early Everglades explorers. They were shot almost to extinction for their feathers (plumes) by the year 1900. The Audubon Society and others helped stopped that ruthless practice and their populations rebounded under protection. But as we settled Florida, we drained the state, put cities and farms on natural habitats, polluted our remaining waters and the plume bird populations crashed again, this time from habitat destruction. We still have about half our wetlands left and plume birds still are seen far and wide, but only about one tenth as many as before.

Great egrets and wood storks (endangered)

An underappreciated part of our spectacular bird life is migratory birds. North America has the highest percent of migratory birds of any continent. Some 250 species of North American birds spend the winter south of the Tropic of Cancer, “neotropical migrants.” And many northern species spend the winter here in Florida. These include the colorful warblers, orioles, tanagers, cuckoos, shorebirds, ducks, and others. And think of Florida’s location and shape, we are the proverbial “neck of the funnel” for migratory birds coming from all across Canada and eastern North America. We funnel and concentrate migrants from a vast continent!

When neotropical migrants leave Florida, they must be prepared to cross the open ocean, yet many weigh only as much as 4 pennies (humming birds only weigh 2 pennies). They fuel their flight by getting fat, fatter than we ever could, they can double their body weight with fat in just a couple weeks. All that fat is their fuel tank for the flight. If they run in to storms or headwinds over vast seas, they cannot stop, they have to have enough fuel to make it. They are tough beyond belief and can fly for days at a time, but it is a dangerous, arduous journey. And since Florida is the last gas station for them it is our responsibility to maintain ecosystems full of food to fatten them. Otherwise they won't make it.

Birds don't just look and sound pretty, they are useful too. Researchers in Missouri put bird-proof tents over trees in a forest and those trees developed insect and caterpillar outbreaks that caused so much leaf loss it stunted their growth compared with un-tented trees right next to them. Tent-less trees grew faster because they were being protected by bug-eating birds. Most of the bug eating birds also are neotropical migrants who have to go south when winter freezes bugs. So, if you are a forester in Pennsylvania, or Canada, you want these birds to come back and protect your trees. You need Florida to protect the Everglades so your helpful little birds can make it south, and back north, successfully.

The good news for Florida's birds is we have embarked on the "Comprehensive Everglades Restoration Plan." The goal is to restore Florida's ecosystems to the extent we can, while also protecting and enhancing water infrastructure for our cities and farms. The Plan is huge, expensive, confusing, and will take decades, even if it proceeds well. Difficult as it is, it is essential to complete. No one wants years like 2016 where harmful algae blooms were raging in Lake Okeechobee and being dumped on masse on hapless coastal estuaries, driving birds and other life away. This was happening at the same time that Florida Bay could not get enough fresh water for its birds and other inhabitants.

And no one wants the fear of water rationing that now is looming now because of drying lakes and rivers, just a few months after the floods. It's not just birds who already are running out of water, it is people too. The Biscayne Aquifer is fed by the Everglades and furnishes drinking water for about one-third of all Floridians in the Palm Beaches to Miami metroplex. When we restore greater water flows to the Everglades—to help birds and fish--we also are nourishing the most important drinking water source in the state.

Florida's future suitability to birds will involve more than big restoration projects. It will be about every nook and cranny of our state that can offer food and shelter for birds, or not. Our rural areas have a surprising amount of natural and semi-natural rangeland, grazed by wandering cattle and great habitats for birds and wildlife.

White ibis and sandpipers

Ranches retain wetlands that catch and clean water before flowing toward our estuaries or replenishing our aquifers. These undeveloped lands are important for us to value and protect for birds, but again, they sustain and economy of food and fiber for people too.

And as more and more people move here, even our sprawling cities can be made better for birds. Instead of a dominance of glass and concrete, we can fill them with trees, bushes and flowers that bring shade, beauty and habitat for the birds and bees. Our future will be what we make of it. I hope will people remember they came to Florida because of its beauty and variety, and steadfastly protect the natural values that make it so special. If birds have trouble thriving in Florida, people will too.

ELEVEN
THE NATIVE BEAUTY OF FLORIDA

GREGORY KRAMER, Ph.D.
DIRECTOR - HORTICULTURE
BOK TOWER GARDENS
LAKE WALES

"Make you the world a bit better and more beautiful because you have lived in it," are the immortal words of Dutch immigrant, Edward W. Bok inspired by the raw beauty of Florida's Iron Mountain 295 feet above sea level that arose in the Pleistocene Era of fluctuating sea levels.

Escaping to Florida from the windswept snowy winters in Pennsylvania, Bok relocated in the 20's to the pristine wilderness on the Lake Wales Ridge. Walking one day in the silent beauty of his surroundings, he envisioned this land as a natural refuge for the replenishment of the human spirit with shaded oak trees, lush gardens, a bird sanctuary and a centerpiece singing Carillon tower. Manifesting his dream, Bok hired architect Frederick Law Olmsted to begin the transformation along this section of Lake Wales ridge that meanders 150 miles through the spine of Florida. He envisioned and created the magnificent Bok Tower Gardens.

In 1929, after five years of construction, the Gardens were completed and dedicated by President Calvin Coolidge as Bok's gift to the American people. Ironically, one year after the formal dedication, Bok was quietly interred beneath the shadow of his beloved singing Carillon tower and next to the Refection Pond; his "most beautiful place."

Today, Bok Tower Gardens is undergoing a major transformation under the tutelage of Director of Horticulture, Greg Kramer. "It was my grandfather who inspired me to become a Horticulturist; he taught me a lot about Nature. He lived in Louisiana then moved to Long island and indulged my curiosity and interests. With his encouragement, I majored in Biology and Botany at the University of Miami. For my Master's Degree, I specialized in the practical application of Environmental Horticulture at the University of Florida. At Bok Tower Gardens, I continue to pursue my interest in how plants heal themselves from disease and related natural world applications in my Doctoral Degree studies which is also at the University Florida. I am also interested in the prolific variety of the butterfly population at the Gardens, their reproductive behavior and coexistence within the complimentary environment of insects and birds. For example, the honeysuckles and other blossoming flowers in the garden attract tiny hummingbirds and establish a symbiotic relationship with insects as their food source. Additionally, many people may not realize it, but every plant produces its own toxins to ward off threatening herbivores. Today, chemists are re-formulating these toxins into fertilizers and pesticides and medicines. In our organic vegetable garden, we use none of these types of products but in our greenhouse where conventional plants mature, we do use fungicides and pesticides to keep the plants from being overtaken by insects."

Kramer is a consummate Biologist and Naturalist. As he strolls through the Pollinator Garden, he stops to point out a Swallowtail Butterfly laying eggs on one of the Spider Wart fennel plants which is ideally suited for its larvae and metamorphosis into a beautiful butterfly.

When Kramer was hired by David Price, former Director of Horticulture at Bok Tower now President, Price was looking for new a project. "Initially, we decided it was a good time to re-design the existing gardens, thus, we hired an architect to develop a plan. The first stage of the design was the creation of an imaginative Children's Garden focusing on the practical application of learning through Nature play."

The Children's Garden is an exploration of a child's curiosity manifested in self-discovery and expression through many Nature projects then sharing those environmental experiences in original Nature performances. It is education at its best," says Kramer.

Bok Tower Gardens also offers other unique opportunities for the time travelers of the next generation. "For students in grades 3-5, in addition to learning about plants, they can learn how to chart the Earth's equinox and solstice using their own compasses and the sundial at the base of the singing tower. They learn from just a 'shadow' how the Earth's orbit can be used to tell the month of the year," adds Kramer. "Bok Tower Gardens is a learning experience for people of all ages." Standing alongside a Pomegranate tree, Kramer observes the smallest details of the garden's anatomical structure in an atmosphere in which he flourishes creating artistry in the natural world. The new Gardens celebrates an intellectual study for visitors and the opportunity to collaborate with Nature in conserving the Native environment.

Opening into a grand vista nearby is a massive revival project "replicating the carved fringes of the Lake Wales Ridge with pathways that lead into canyons of color and flowing streams. Visitors can experience Nature's artwork from over a million years ago when the upheaval of Florida's limestone platform created rugged caverns and stepping stone cavities that carved through the heart of the peninsula. Today, visitors can hike along the rim of the Lake Wales Ridge on the Pineridge Trail at the eastern edge of the Gardens. It is a visitor's wonderland of Native Florida scrub in a thriving xeriscape of insects, gopher tortoises, sand hill cranes, scrub blue jays, wild turkeys, and snakes. Bok Tower Gardens Volunteer Guide, Pete Brockman, leads hikes along the Ridge and tells the story of Native Florida while visitors enjoy the cacophony of crickets, song birds, and the provocative silence of the Natural world.

Meandering through the Gardens is a transition from various ecosystems unfolding and blending into the landscape of the next. "We strive to create an aesthetic appreciation throughout the Gardens including the Arid Plain with tall oaks and ground covering wire grass transitioning into the Wet Plains. We support Native ecology and the landscape that expresses Florida's natural habitat and beauty, perpetuating Bok's vision in the 1920's."

"On the Sandhill or Arid Plain, we have amended the soil of the white sugar sand which is the perfect environment for the restoration of the long leaf pine," says Kramer.

"Each ecosystem provides the soil environment for different types of native plants to grow and where we can create an 'aesthetic' appreciation for visitors to enjoy. There is the 'Wet Prairie' that also grows majestic pines surrounding the quiet beauty and harmonious serenity of a pond where visitors can pause and reflect in silence and beauty. In the mornings, I come here to the Window by the Pond and read visitor comments about their experience," says Kramer.

One of the most unique attractions developed in collaboration with the University of Florida is the Outdoor and Edible Kitchen Garden. In raised beds, there are "cucurbitaceaes" or gourd plants, such as cucumbers, eggplant and other vegetables such eggplant, red cabbage, okra, and elderberry. "Alongside the vegetables, we plant marigolds whose roots inhibit nematodes."

The Kitchen Garden features local Chefs creating a sampling of artistic and favorable creations for visitors grown in the organic edible garden including Pizza Plants and a special "Salsa" in the "Fresh Bites" series.

Since the University of Florida has partnered with Bok Tower Gardens this collaboration provides new insights into Nature's processes and offers the opportunity to create new plant varieties which Kramer incorporates into the Kitchen and Outdoor Gardens including the Florida peach adapted to flourish in this environment. There are also hybrid persimmons, papaya, and heirloom sugar cane originating in Africa. At the Kitchen Gardens, visitors can see a demonstration of how tough-hided sugar cane is processed into refined sugar. The UF also collaborates with local Florida farmers to create a wide variety of grapes that we grow in the Gardens including a table grape that can be infused with Florida's native Muscadine Grape to process into local Florida wine," Kramer explains.

At the nearby Blue Moon Café, nestled within a peaceful cove of the landscape, they offer a unique menu including some of the delectable organic edible plant dishes from the garden, as well as traditional lunch specialties. Creative Chefs prepare lunch with fresh black berries, raspberries comingled with yogurt, vegetable salads, a hearty selection of sandwiches and a variety of dishes to awaken the taste buds. The Cafe offers home brewed tea, sodas, a culinary selection of wines and beers from around the world. The total kitchen garden covers approximately a quarter of an acre," says Kramer.

Kramer's expanded awareness of the natural world at Bok Tower has expanded into an international adventure recently returning from Cuba on a sponsored program by the Native Plant Society. "Cuba has one of the largest botanical gardens in the world. They grow organic tobacco, soaking the leaves in neonicotinoids to cure into tobacco. Yes, it is true the Cubans grow organic tobacco but they derive the nicotinoids from soaking leaves in water and spraying the water soaked in leaves to control insects. Neonicotinoids are a new class of nicotinoids that are re-formulated and can't be used in organic production. This process has nothing to do with curing tobacco, only controlling pests."

"One of the Cuban Horticulturists also pointed out that the nearly extinct Ivory Billed Woodpecker may make its home on the eastern side of the island. That was a conversation with a Naturalist I had during a bird walk in a nature preserve, when he said that the Ivory Billed Woodpecker may reside among some of the natural woodlands in the mountains on the eastern side of the island. The bird is not found at the Garden. It is such a rare bird that if the bird does still exist almost nobody will admit to it."

Since the Cuban Revolution in 1959 when Castro took over Cuba from Battista, "Cuba is now hosting private industry," says Kramer "but 90 percent of the government still owns all the agriculture with a 10 percent ownership by Native residents. If a farmer grows a crop of vegetables, they have to give 90 percent of their profit to the Cuban government. However, at the present time, there is a horticultural dialogue taking shape. The Cuban people in the field are very knowledgeable. They grow Casaba or Yucca, which is a popular food in the U.S. and Cuba, as well as sugar cane from which they make aged rum. At the hotel where we stayed, we ate a lot of fresh fruit such as mangoes and papaya but no beef," said Kramer. According to Cuban history, when Castro took over Cuba he had all the beef slaughtered and handed it out to the people who had been deprived of beef under Battista's regime. However, Kramer says he would like to initiate a collaborative horticulture mission between the U.S. and Cuba. The Cuban government allows tours of the island and specialty trips through T.R.E.E (The Florida Keys Tropical Research Ecological Exchange Institute, Key West, Florida).

Kramer is a keen observer wherever his explorations take him. "One time when I was a Highlands Hammock State Park in Sebring, I observed a very touching scene. A lady was embracing the ancient base of an old thousand-year giant Oak and whispering a fond greeting: 'It is so good to see you again my old friend!'" Just as the unknown lady, Greg Kramer lives in the arms of Nature.

Today, Bok Tower Gardens welcomes millions of visitors from

around the world, each person passes through the overarching portals into the Visitors Center framing Bok's memorable words:

"Make you the world a bit better or more beautiful because you have lived in it."

TWELVE

C&B FARMS, INC.

FRESH FAMILY PRODUCE

ORGANIC AND CONVENTIONAL

AGRICULTURE

CHUCK OBERN, PRESIDENT

CLEWISTON

With 30 years in agricultural farming and science, Chuck Obern, President of C&B Farms, Clewiston, Florida, and his son, Charles, Jr., or "Boots," have earned a widespread reputation across the U.S. for consistent quality and management as growers of organic and conventional agricultural specialty produce. With the increase in consumer demand for organics, Obern says "It has been a long time coming but we now harvest more than fifty types of organic and conventional vegetables including basil, thyme, eggplant, watermelons, and more."

Obern's interest in agriculture was spurred after his college days at American University, Washington D. C. "I realized I couldn't stand academics, so I quit and got a 'no frills' minimum wage job at a local nursery." It was a turning point in Obern's career. Driven by personal ambition and nurtured by his father's encouragement to go beyond academic success, young Obern forged his own path.

As Obern learned about plants and how to keep them healthy, he became a valued nursery employee. The company decided to support his enthusiasm and offered him the use of the company's greenhouse to cultivate plants; Obern enthusiastically seized the opportunity. After a year of hard work, he was well-anointed in horticulture but realized he needed more scientific research to forge ahead.

Dr. Mason Marvel, who knew the Obern family when they lived in the exotic trappings of Kuala Lumpar, recommended that Oberon enroll, full-time, in the agricultural program at University of Florida. Working his way through, he had the opportunity to assist professors with their scientific research freeing him to explore and learn more about the complex world of plants. Obern's academic success, this time around, was fueled by heightened interest and he made the President's straight "A "list of outstanding students at UF. Now, it was time to turn another page in his career.

With only three credits to go before graduation, Obern was hired by a grower in LaBelle and earned his last credits working in the field. Obern said "It wasn't the 'sheepskin' that mattered to him but the gratification of incorporating academics into practical applications." He created innovative agricultural practices that involved improving quality of fruits/vegetables, creating new variations, and streamlining production. Then, in 1986, another opportunity arose as Obern was offered a share in a piece of land to part-time farm vegetables. This was the birth of C&B Farms.

Starting from scratch in this new commercial venture, Obern initiated a nutrition and disease prevention plan. "Plants produce their own natural pesticides which today are synthetically modified, applied in the field to control infestations of insects and disease and stimulate the plant's immunity system which results in more efficient utilization of nutrients increasing production of food/fiber yields essential for economic success."

Mike Counts, C&B Sales Manager who has worked 20 years at various organic and conventional agriculture companies says, "When I came to work at C&B, we launched an expansive marketing plan to grocery stories/commercial markets, integrating applied academic practices with established procedures and experimental applications to increase production and income."

"We run a tight production schedule," says Counts. "Nothing grows year-round, so we start planting in August and harvest October through June, the growing season may last 30 to 120 days depending on the crop grown. When our produce is harvested, it is shipped within 24 hours with a ceiling of 36 hours to arrive at its destination. In the meantime, we continue to mulch and weed. There is no down time in the agricultural business. Presently, we grow more than fifty types of conventional and organic vegetables on 2,500 acres with $18 million dollars in sales."

Driving through the Farm, the symmetrical rows of lush collards, corn, cucumbers, squash cabbage, beets, eggplant, cucumbers, bell peppers, organic marjoram, mint, cilantro, parsley, rosemary and many more are planted. "We use plastic sheets to hold in the water on some of our raised beds," says Obern. "Quality is emphasized in every phase of our production and all of our produce is sold before it is planted."

Obern (father and son) personally oversee the entire operation along with a trusted team of employees who know their job, company requirements and state/federal regulations. "Every week, Counts, Tommy Armata, also in sales, and I hold a meeting with team leaders to assess quality and growing procedures, pesticide application, fertilization, harvesting, soil regeneration and the time table for planting. We do on site composting, shipping in horse manure from a large Boca Raton Racetrack to amend the soil and stabilize continuous enrichment inducing growth of the crops." Obern adds that "horse manure has no pesticide residue and after composting, no pathogens."

In today's commodity market, agriculture is based on "economy of scale." High-end customers who purchase organic fruits and vegetables look for the USDA "Certified Organic" label at the grocery store. Organic producers/packers must meet specific USDA accreditation and requirements for growing fruits and vegetables. "There must be no pesticides, chemical fertilizers or dyes used and the produce must not be processed using industrial solvents: biological control of insects is acceptable," explains Obern. According to the USDA, the goal of organic farming is to integrate culture, biological, and mechanical practices into food production that fosters cycling resources, promotes ecological balance, and conserves biodiversity. Obern adds that "organic, however, is a perception, as some herbicides were originally discovered from plants and some soil micro-organisms. The public is not informed about what is organic and not organic, as organics are not pesticide free. Neem oil is naturally derived from a seed as the tree has a natural chemical defense that is toxic and repels insects. However, some naturally produced toxins cannot be used in organics. For example, nicotine is natural but it is toxic if consumed by humans and cannot be used on edible crops. Government regulations determine what is considered to be organic or conventional."

What is important in growing organics? Obern says it "has to do with how we 'feed' our plants. We use natural fertilizer, such as chicken feathers, meal, and natural potassium sulfate such as potassium from the sea. We also use compost on the organic crops for soil amendment. Farmers/packers products are reviewed by a third party, accredited by the USDA, for quality assurance and certification. The Environmental Protection Agency (EPA) sets maximum tolerant safety levels for every pesticide, both organic and conventional."

Another agricultural concern in the U.S. is the threat of competition from cheaper and less quality imported produce. "In America, we are financially liable for safe food production. We should require all foreign agricultural importers to hold money as a security bond if their product is determined to be harmful so the American consumer is protected; however, that is considered to be an impediment to trade by some. In Florida, we need better vigilance over imported produce as we import fifty percent of our produce from Mexico and other countries. Even though it is monitored by the USDA, some of the illegal drugs are packed and shipped in produce," says Obern.

Since C&B is proud of their locally grown produce, bringing it to market is more costly. "The wholesale and retail price is affected by higher transportation and carbon miles; but people want a 'fresh taste.' Competition from foreign markets results in a 30-50% disparity in price between U.S. grown and cheaper imported produce. Forty percent of our cost is for labor which is a big difference compared to the cost of foreign labor. It is difficult to match imported food prices as they don't have the same growing restrictions or labor charges. In the United States, the price of wholesale vegetables generally decreases at the end of the month due to the biggest payer, the U.S. Government, for entitlement programs at the beginning of the month."

"In commercial agriculture in the U.S., it is an economic challenge every year and each year is different," states Obern, however, he emphatically adds, "It our dedication, as commercial growers, to produce quality crops to preserve future generations."

THIRTEEN

"WHO IS TO BLAME FOR SOUTH FLORIDA'S ENVIRONMENTAL PROBLEMS?"

GUEST CONTRIBUTOR: KATRINA ELSKEN INDEPENDENT NEWS MEDIA FLORIDA

In the summer of 2016, a thick, massive algae bloom covered much of the Indian River Lagoon.

On television news programs, coastal residents blamed the Army Corps of Engineers and the South Florida Water Management District. But both are government agencies following the water management policies set by elected officials or in the case of SFWMD, a board appointed by an elected official.

On the TV news, people repeated the claim that the problem was due to releases from Lake Okeechobee, although scientific studies conducted by the University of Florida and Harbor Branch

Oceanographic Institute found the freshwater lake releases are just a small part of the problem.

Some people wanted to blame agriculture, although due to the dairy buyout in the 1980s, the agriculture north of the lake is mostly low impact, such as cattle ranches with thousands of acres of native pasture. And since water does not run uphill and back pumping of agricultural runoff into the lake had been banned, nutrient impact from agriculture south of the lake is minimal.

So, who was really to blame?

Let's take a survey:

• If you live and/or have a farm, business or industry in South Florida — say anywhere from Orlando south — raise your hand. Ask any biologist who studies lakes and rivers.

Anytime a human enters an ecosystem, it changes. The more humans, the more change. The University of Florida Water Institute Report explains: "An extensive network of man-made canals, levees and water control structures permeates the south Florida landscape. The land has been ditched, drained and otherwise reconfigured to provide flood protection and fresh water for a current population of more than eight million residents." Every time any of those humans build a house, school or shopping mall or pave a road or a parking lot, it changes the natural flow of water. And those 8 million residents produce waste that goes into the environment.

Because that population keeps growing, so do the problems.

- If you didn't vote in the last election, because you were too busy, or you forgot or you don't want to be called for jury duty (despite the fact that Florida no longer uses the voter list for juries), raise your hand.
- If you have a septic tank and do not have it pumped and inspected at least once every five years, raise your hand. Septic tanks that do not operate properly contribute to excess nutrients in the runoff entering area waterways.
- If your home is on a city sewer system and you never wondered where it goes when you flush, raise your hand. This is especially important if you live in the Indian River Lagoon Basin, where the population has swelled from 250,000 in 1960 to 1.7 million people today. Anyone who lives on the Treasure Coast should read the Harbor Branch Oceanographic Institute study, "Evidence of sewage-driven eutrophication and harmful algal blooms in Florida's Indian River Lagoon"
- If you have planted anything in your yard that requires fertilizer, raise your hand. Rain washes fertilizer into waterways, contributing to the excess nutrient load.

- If you enjoy visiting the Orlando area theme parks, raise your hand. The development in the Kissimmee and Orlando area with theme parks, hotels, restaurants, roads, etc., required drainage and flood control and that means water comes down the Kissimmee Chain of Lakes into the Kissimmee River and down the river into the lake much faster than nature intended. Water enters the lake six times faster than it can be released. It starts to stack up against the dike — an earthen berm that was built for flood control, not for water storage. Some areas on the south end of the dike are less than 12 feet above sea level. If the lake's water level were to be 17 or 18 or 19 feet, and the dike breached, expect loss of life in the resulting flooding.
- Unless you raise all of your own food organically and make sure no runoff ever leaves your property, raise your hand. Although it is not the main culprit, agricultural runoff does contribute to the excess nutrients in the watershed.

But without agriculture, there would be no food. It is also important to note that the farmers have already made a lot of sacrifices to clean up the water.

For example, in the mid-1980s, new regulations forced most of the dairy industry out of the watershed. The few remaining dairies in Okeechobee County are required to recycle their own runoff and contain and clean up the water on their property.

OK, I could go on, but it's getting difficult to type with one hand raised, and you get the idea …

Whose fault are the environmental problems in the South Florida watershed?

There's plenty of blame to go around for every resident, every visitor, every farm, every business and every industry in south Florida.

Who will it take to fix the problem? All of us.

What can you do to help solve the problems?

- You can support legislation to provide more water storage both north and south of Lake Okeechobee, as well as more water storage in the Caloosahatchee and St. Lucie basins. Water storage to the north will help slow the flow into the lake and allow natural vegetation to clean the water before it enters the lake. That's good for the health of the lake, and good for every area that receives water from the lake. It also helps store water that might be needed in the dry season, instead of sending it to tide. Storage in the Caloosahatchee and St. Lucie basins will do the same for those basins. In addition, storage in the Caloosahatchee basin will provide a source of water for the river in the dry season, to help prevent salt water intrusion.
- You can do your homework during the election cycle and find out which candidates will support plans to clean up the environmental problems. Then you can vote. Then you can

continue to hold your elected officials accountable by staying involved.

- You can plant "Florida Friendly" plants in your own yard. And you can resist the urge to water your Florida grass and instead just let it go brown during the dry season because it will come back, as nature intended, when the rains come. For more on Florida Friendly landscapes contact your county extension office.
- You can keep runoff on your own property by using a retention pond, or by just putting up with a soggy yard part of the year. That water is recharging your aquifer.
- You can clean up after yourself. Don't throw trash, cans or bottles into the water, canals or shorelines.
- If you catch "trash" fish like armored catfish, you can take them with you and dispose of them properly. Don't just leave them on the canal bank.
- If your home has a septic tank, you can have it serviced regularly to make sure it is operating properly and not leaching nutrients and bacteria into runoff from your

property. And if it is failing, it should be replaced (or have your home hooked up to a public sewer system, if that is an option in your area.)

- If you live in an area with a sewer system, you can pressure local elected officials to make sure the sewer systems are kept up properly and not allowed to leach sewage into the groundwater or runoff.
- If you have an RV, you can make sure you only dump your "black water" at designated stations. Never dump onto a road or canal. And if you see another RVer dumping, report them. They are polluting everyone's water.
- Instead of complaining about the problem and looking for someone or something to blame, you can be part of the solution.

Contact Information:

kelsken@newszap.com

Airboats in the Everglades

FOURTEEN
RETURN TO NATURE: THE KISSIMMEE RIVER RESTORATION

LOISA KERWIN, DIRECTOR
RIVERWOODS FIELD LAB
CORNWELL

Today, the beautiful, restored Kissimmee River winds its way through the natural beauty of Central Florida's lush wetland landscapes, flushed with colorful waterfowl, alligators hunkered down along the banks, and turtles perched on snags along the river's edge and busy insects clustered on glorious blooming plants.

The Kissimmee River's pathway south begins at the Chain of

Lakes in the greater Orlando area and carves its way through wetlands and cattle country to discharge into the northern shores of Lake Okeechobee at Okee-tantie County Park on Highway 78. The Kissimmee River's history reveals years of extreme flooding and drought. In the 1960s, in response to many wet years, the Army Corp of Engineers was charged with channelizing and straightening the natural curves of the Kissimmee River to provide flood protection for the growing communities in the Orlando region. From 1962-71, the 103 meandering miles of the Kissimmee River was transformed into the C-38 canal – a 30-foot-deep, 300 feet wide, 56-mile-long drainage ditch that provided a solution to the flooding. However, what they did not realize is that the wildlife and water quality in the Kissimmee and Lake Okeechobee would rapidly decline. The bass fisheries, a long time economic driver in the region, crashed. The sharp trills of songbirds were silenced, their nests abandoned, and their food supply vanished in the river's degraded waters.

Residents and users of the Kissimmee River soon realized that draining the wetlands and converting them in pasture and dry prairie was an environmental disaster!! By 1992, due to public outcry for environmental accountability, the Kissimmee River Restoration Project (KRRP) was authorized by Congress. The state is investing millions of dollars in the Kissimmee River and Everglades Restoration projects to help restore and protect what is left of Florida's valuable resources.

Riverwoods Field Lab is the base of operations for the Kissimmee River Restoration Project – a 50/50 project between the US Army Corps of Engineers and the South Florida Water Management District (SFWMD). The SFWMD has a long-standing partnership with Florida Atlantic University's (FAU) Center for Environmental Studies (CES) to manage Riverwoods as an Education and Research Center. The team at Riverwoods works closely with the SFWMD to provide research support and educational opportunities for Florida's residents and students, as well as national and international audiences.

At the helm of Riverwoods is visionary, Loisa Kerwin, Asst. Director of Florida Atlantic University's Center for Environmental Studies, a young Florida pioneer. **The Riverwoods Field Lab** headquarters is nestled in a wedge of beauty along the river's shores on Highway 98 in Cornwell, Florida. The Lab, shaded beneath arching moss laden oaks, is a safe haven for nature's creatures and nature lovers, research scientists and students. Kerwin has served as Riverwoods Director for 16 years and worked for FAU's Center for Environmental Studies (CES) for 20 years. She says, "I truly love my job – it is always an adventure working with students, teachers, faculty and scientists. I have an extremely talented team and we work together to achieve our common goal of helping educate people about the importance of protecting our natural environment."

The Kissimmee River Restoration Project (KRRP) began in 1999, and is scheduled to be completed in 2019. The KRRP will restore the form and function of the middle third of the historic, meandering Kissimmee River. So far, 3 out of the 5 restoration construction Phases have been successfully completed restoring approx. 24 miles of meandering river. The 4th Phase backfilling the C-38, south of the Highway 98 bridge, is currently underway. The 5th and final restoration Phase has started. The river's populations of aquatic invertebrates, game fish, wading birds, and waterfowl have returned to their "old friend" for shelter and food. Ultimately, when the project is completed, there will be 22 miles of the C-38 canal filled in, restoring 43 miles of meandering river and reestablishing approx. 13,000 acres of wetlands. There will be 4 water control structures (damns) at the top and bottom of the river that will remain to provide flood protection for communities north and south of the river.

Kerwin feels that students should be aware of Florida's environmental issues, so Riverwoods uses the Kissimmee River Restoration as a model of an extremely successful project. "In our **Student Field Studies Program**", Kerwin says, "We strive to excite students about Florida's natural resources using hands-on, environmental science as the "hook"." Kerwin says, "We want students to be aware of our environmental issues, understand human's impacts, and ultimately, help preserve what we have left."

"We immerse students in restoration ecology and teach them how to collect data and conduct field science including:

- Dip netting for aquatic invertebrates and fish
- Completing diversity and abundance bird surveys
- Testing water quality, and
- Identifying native and invasive wetland plants

Through our programs and actions, we show students how they can help make a difference!" Kerwin emphasizes.

"Riverwoods is designed as a 'living lab' with Student Field Study programs that are available for middle, high school and college students with a focus of STEM education (science, technology, engineering and math). These unique opportunities attract teachers and faculty from all over Florida that want to enhance their students' environmental knowledge and science literacy. Riverwoods programs offer an exciting opportunity to explore and protect nature in the heart of Florida's expanding development and agriculture," Kerwin explains.

"Students interested in environmental science or recreational activities such as fishing, hunting, boating and bird watching have many opportunities for environmental careers in the Florida," says Kerwin. One of the Kissimmee scientists, Brent Anderson, Herpetologist, has worked ten years with the South Florida Water Management District, shares his enjoyment of the project as he says he gets "a chance to capture and observe unique reptiles and amphibians usually undetected through traditional survey methods." He says that he has transformed his career dreams into reality. Sharing his enthusiasm with students, he inspires them to pursue a career in environmental science.

A fascinating component of the Field Lab studies is Eco-tours. Kerwin says, "The Explorer II program is designed for young people and adults beginning with a floating science lesson aboard the beautiful 30-foot pontoon boat that brings participants into a world of Nature's mysteries.

In charge of steering the passengers to curious destinations along the river is US Coast Guard Certified Masters Captain, Mark Compeau, who carefully maneuvers the pontoon research vessel into wildlife habitat without disturbing it, as he stops to point out nesting fish or birds along the bank.

"We have very environmentally friendly residents in Highlands County that love to learn about our environmental resources and projects," says Kerwin. "We offer fee-based Eco-tours for up to 17 guests for any organizations that are interested. Every year, we work with Highlands County Audubon and host several field trips during the birding season. Any group is welcome - home owners associations, church groups and garden clubs.

One of the unique adult education opportunities provided by Riverwoods are **Art in Nature** workshops. Recently, Riverwoods Field Lab hosted a Yoga Retreat with participants from all over Florida who came to relax aboard the pontoon boat for a day of serenity, to enjoy a special interpretive tour of the River with Loisa Kerwin and returning to the peaceful homage of the lab for a revitalizing Yoga practice led by instructor, Dr. Nancy Dale. The beauty of the day ended as the shadow of a golden sunset melted into the River. It was a time to be remembered. The Yoga Retreat is a continuing program, not only for those immersed in Yoga, but for anyone who wants to share a day in Nature. "If you like cruising on a comfortable pontoon boat to count birds and relax on the river, then come see us in one of Highlands County's best kept secrets – Exploring the Kissimmee River at Riverwoods Field Lab," adds Kerwin.

"As the final phase of the Restoration project takes effect, it is monitored for evidence of renewed life along the River," Kerwin explains. "The ultimate result is the transformation of a 'dead river' channelized as a solution for flood prevention into the revitalized beauty of the original Kissimmee River with its gentle meandering flow, restored water quality and the return of abundant wildlife. The Kissimmee River Restoration and the Riverwoods Field Lab is making a positive impact on Native Florida for many generations in the future. **For more information about Riverwoods Programs online: www.ces.fau.edu/riverwoods**

Photo: Jennifer Swain, Editor

FIFTEEN
THREATS TO THE SURVIVAL OF FISHEATING CREEK

GUEST CONTRIBUTOR: PAULA HOUSE
ATTORNEY AND EXECUTIVE DIRECTOR OF SAVE OUR CREEKS, INC.

{VIEWS EXPRESSED HERE ARE SOLELY THOSE OF THE CONTRIBUTING AUTHOR)

Coming eye to eye with an alligator and living to tell the story is a rare occurrence anywhere in the world, but it is common on Fisheating Creek. For years, the local public and environmental organizations have fought to keep the Creek running free into Lake Okeechobee with access to the public. Those efforts have paid off, as the Creek remains one of the wildest places in Florida, where the natural environment of Old Florida still exists.

Since 1999, when Florida acquired the Creek in Glades County, there have been many projects that would challenge both the free flow of the creek into Lake Okeechobee and the headwaters in Highlands County. No less than three major construction developments threatened the future of the Creek in Highlands County. As with the original acquisition, local residents and organizations hired lawyers and fought the projects, both at the state and levels. The citizens were successful in halting all three projects.

On the Glades side, another kind of lawsuit has been going on to prevent the state from eradicating a navigational channel that runs through Cowbone Marsh. I am happy to say that, as of the writing of this article, the citizens have prevailed in court to keep the potential for navigation of the entire 52 miles of the creek possible.

But there is a new threat to the natural state of Fisheating Creek. It comes from the special interests of the Everglades Agricultural Area and South Florida Water Management District, which has become an arm of the policy preferences of Governor Scott. Scott's plan will back up yet more water in Lake Okeechobee rather than sending the water south, as has been recognized as proper environmental solution to the havoc caused by the extreme variations in rainfall.

South Florida Water Management District (SFWMD) is moving quickly to identify projects to store, hold or permanently dispose of Lake Okeechobee water that is contributing to the undesirable discharges to the Caloosahatchee and St. Lucie estuaries. At a meeting September 21, 2016, SFWMD unveiled strategies that included massive reservoirs for Glades County between the Brighton Reservation eastern boundary line and Route 78. The reservoir or a combination of reservoirs would hold at a minimum 250,000 acre feet of water. SFWMD also proposed aquifer storage and recovery wells (ASR), deep well injection (DWI), and restoration of wetlands and littoral zones between the Lake and the reservoirs. All projects have the goal of being located as close as possible to Lake Okeechobee.

According to Lisa Aley, the Army Corps of Engineers, projects or "features" have been chosen based on their capacity to hold water. Using projections from modeling technology and formulas, she recommended a reservoir south of the Kissimmee River between the Brighton Reservation eastern boundary and Route 78 to a point approximately half way to Fisheating Creek. This reservoir would hold 263,504 acre feet of water and is designated as reservoir K-05. The second-best option would require two reservoirs that combined would store 248,822 acre feet of water. One reservoir, I-01, would locate south of the proposed K-05 reservoir, between Brighton Reservation and Route 78 and end just above Lakeport. A second reservoir, K-42, near Lake Istokpoga, would be needed to achieve the storage goal and both would be built if the second option is chosen.

In addition to the reservoirs, water would be stored or disposed of in wells. Between 30 and 80 ASR and DWI wells are proposed. Water injected into DWI wells cannot be recovered, while water down ASR wells can be withdrawn if needed. Possible locations for the these wells include the C-41 and C-40 canals, Paradise Run, outflow of the Kissimmee River, Taylor Creek, Lakeside Ranch and Port Mayaca.

The projects will have an impact on Glades County and the Brighton Reservation, from significant changes to landscape and hydrology north of Lakeport to the uncertainty about drinking water quality from underground storage of contaminated water from Lake Okeechobee and the watershed.

The project is also a foot in the door to control and confiscation of the waters flowing from Fisheating Creek. One of the favored reservoirs is just north of Fisheating Creek Bay, from Lakeport to about half way to the Kissimmee River outlet.

The local public has participated in some of the meetings that have been called to promote the project. There is, as yet no formal opposition. But from the comments at the meeting, that opposition does not seem far away. At a meeting September 21, 2017, one participant asked if the new projects complied with goals and requirements of existing projects under the Comprehensive Everglades Restoration Plan (CERP). For instance, a "water savings clause" under in a regulation adopted in 2000 may not allow for disposal of water down DWI wells that cannot be recovered or other measures that may affect water right. Another participant lamented that wells were nothing but "vertical canals," and said the plan did not represent progress towards healing Florida's water problems.

So, for how much longer will you be able to meet a gator in the eye on Fisheating Creek and live to tell about. That is anyone's guess.

Meeting materials, maps showing the proposed projects and other information on the Lake Okeechobee Watershed Project are available at http://www.saj.usace.army.mil/Missions/Environmental/Ecosystem-Restoration/Lake-Okeechobee-Watershed-Project/.

SIXTEEN

"THE ANCIENT ART OF HIDE TANNING"

DOUG SMITH

SEBRING

Tanning animal hides is an ancient art dating back to 7000 B.C. when the Sumerians pounded hides into leather for use on their giant chariot wheels. The process of drying an animal's skin in those days was a labor-intensive process, as it is today, that began by removing hair, flesh and fat then soaking it in water, urine and other natural compounds to stretch it, dry it out for months before removing, by hand with a knife, any remaining hair. After it was dry, the ancients pounded it out, even using their feet to knead the skin. After the skin was sufficiently stretched, oils were applied to create a finished leather product, using any leftover leather to make glue.

In the natural environment thousands of years ago to the present, animals had a multipurpose usefulness. When animals were slaughtered for food on the farm or in the 1800's at a Florida slaughterhouse, every part of the carcass was used for practical purposes. Fur hides provided warmth; hides were used for rugs, leather for belts, bindings, jewelry, shoes and other utilitarian items. Doug Smith, Sebring, Florida Hide Tanner says the process "has not changed very much from the past."

"What I do to process hides is to first salt it heavily about a quarter of an inch over the entire hide, fold it in half and place it on a sheet of plywood at an angle to the ground; this pulls any natural fluids out and sets the hair. The next day, I shake off the salt and repeat this step. Next. I rinse the hide in clear water and add a couple drops of dawn dish soap. I swish the hide around for a few minutes and rinse it completely to remove all soap. I then mix up a batch of pickle solution depending on the size of the hide, most skins can be done in a five-gallon bucket. I mix one gallon of water with one gallon of vinegar and add two cups of salt. I soak the hide in this solution for three days being sure to stir it twice a day. Next, I give the hide a quick rinse and drape it over something to drain while I make the tan. If the pickle looks good it can be used, just add two ounces of Alum and, if you have the ability, check the pH of the solution, it should be three or four. Soak the hide in this solution for one or two days again being sure to stir it twice a day."

"Next, I take the hide out, rinse it and again drape it over something to drain while I make the furriers oil. I use hand lotion mixed with an equal amount of water and a small amount of added glycerin. I lay the hide out flat on a sheet of plywood with the hair down and spread the furriers oil on the flesh side. Then, I fold the skin in half and let the oil soak in overnight. The next day, I open the hide and begin the drying process in the shade and check the hide daily by gently stretching it. When I see it has changed color and can visibly tell it is drying I become more aggressive in the stretching. Once the hide is completely dry and stretched it may be sanded which will help soften it even more. It is now ready for use. If you just want a rug or wall hanging there is no need to manually stretch it, just tack it out flat to a sheet of plywood and let it dry.

Smith became a Hide Tanner through the back door, growing up in a cosmopolitan environment on Merritt Island, where his dad worked for NASA's space program, designing guidance and control systems. "My dad grew up on a farm but once he left, he only returned to see his mother and vacation; he did not encourage his children to be farmers," says Smith.

"I wanted to become an artist but my dad steered me towards Veterinarian Medicine which I showed an interest in till my early 30's. Although I learned a lot about modern technology and sciences, I was interested most in the Life Sciences and learning the old-world methods of doing things. I pursued this interest at the University of Florida, graduating with a degree in Microbiology and Chemistry. Many years later, I earned a Master's Degree in Health Care Administration," Smith explains.

Presently, Smith works in Histology (the study of tissues) for a gastroenterology group. Smith says, "Scientists first learned about Histology by studying hide tanning." As part of Smith's dual interest, he says, "I also make wine, as winemaking involves microbiology. Yeast is a bacterium which ferments sugar into alcohol and determines the sweet taste or dryness of wine. Winemaking ties in with hide tanning of animals/reptiles as it also involves a natural way to process grapes or fruit," Smith adds.

"Living natural" is Smith's philosophy and way of life. "I have a garden and grow my own food. I raise chickens and turkeys for eggs and goats for meat and their skins. (Although many people do milk goats, as it is healthier than cows' milk, I prefer to let the kids have that). I prefer to slaughter farm animals for food. Many of the animal or reptile hides I use for tanning come from 'road kill,'" says Smith.

"I design and customize many types of products from leather but I am not concerned with tanning leather for the car industry or for other commercial applications. I make alligator wallets, reptile specialty items and bring a number of tanned hides and custom made by-products, including fur skins, to sell at the Conservation Corps Celebration every year in the Fall at Highlands Hammock State Park and other Pioneer festivals. This also gives me the opportunity to talk to people about the art and practice of hide tanning, as today more people are distanced from the land and a natural lifestyle. I am the only one of four brothers who chose to live off the native land as each of them chose to live a cosmopolitan lifestyle."

"Living natural is off the grid," says Smith "but it also means conserving resources and becoming economically independent. My dad went through the 1930's Depression and stressed being prepared for the possibility of another one. I live off the land that provides me with food and other resources for the animals. I am not dependent on the grocery store to purchase processed food."

"For people who want to become economically independent," Smith suggests, "buying land and growing your own food. For city dwellers, individuals can learn how to grow a hydroponic roof garden, preserving the fruits of their labor through canning. Other ways to create a stable food production is by making dried beef jerky in your own kitchen which is far tastier than store bought processed jerky," Smith says.

"For conservation of water on my property, I pump fresh water from an underground well using an old fashioned "pitcher pump"," Smith explains. Living a natural lifestyle requires discipline and responsibility and is a very labor intensive alternative lifestyle for food production unlike the commercial cosmopolitan cooking regimen of ripping open a package and microwaving its contents. "Living off the land is a healthier discipline and economical. Living and working the land meets my human needs and my spiritual values," reiterates Smith. "I embrace life."

SEVENTEEN

21ST CENTURY WILDERNESS MAN

GREG JOHNSON

PALMDALE

Born in Arcadia, Florida, Jan 20, 1977, 38-year-old Greg Johnson has created a life in the wilds of Palmdale, living in small three room wooden solar powered house, living "off the grid" with a "pitcher pump" for water and an outside latrine.

Greg Johnson has been a man of Nature all his life and is now living his dream. Unlike most young men his age who "visit" the woods, he has adopted Nature and Nature has adopted him. All his life, Johnson has explored the Everglades, hiked in the woods, fished, discovering new adventures that most people only imagine. He is now living a free-spirit lifestyle outside the norm. He has chosen to live amongst wildlife in a deserted wilderness with Fisheating Creek running through his back yard. He swims in the Creek with alligators and moccasins.

Johnson has chosen this way of life and lives his philosophy, "If you take care of Nature, Nature will take care of you." He has been a day worker cowboy for Lykes Brothers in Glades County further initiating him into the rustic environment. As he says, "Just like a woman, Palmdale stole his heart." Johnson is a "romantic" surrounded by ancient oaks sleeping under a blanket of stars with the melodious cacophony of crickets lulling him to sleep every night.

Greg Johnson is a Landscape Architect, driving more than 100 miles to Naples where he began his independent business in 2002 when he worked for ranchers living in remote Immokalee, near the Florida panther reserve. Johnson says driving along highway 850, he got rare glimpses of the native cat, slinking along the roadside.

Johnson is an explorer and adventurer. He expanded his vision of Native culture when he moved from Immokalee to Palmdale. He first rented a small lot at Ray Hendry's Campground furthering his journey of discovery in the small town with a fluctuating population of 300-400 people nestled along the bank of one of the last pristine rivers in Florida: Fisheating Creek.

"When I first settled in Palmdale, I met one of Palmdale's locals, Ray Hendry, who took me over to the deserted property of longtime resident recluse, Lucky Whidden. Whidden is a Palmdale legend. Whidden's self-made home burned down but the arch above the entrance remained and welcomed friends into "Lucky's Ponderosa." "You can still see the remains of the small walkway across the front yard that led to Lucky Whidden's two room house. When I first visited Lucky's property," says Johnson, "I was met with old cars and swamp buggies left behind by Lucky who made a living repairing everything from cars to plumbing, out of his well-equipped garage, every spare part neatly stowed along the walls. Lucky's small house, by design, had a living room possessing only a sofa, TV, and a little coffee table beside his favorite chair with a well-worn groove where he lodged his beer bottle. One day when the author was visiting Lucky, he pulled out from underneath the sofa a box of old "golden books" saved from his childhood. As we were reading some of the stories, a couple of rugged cowboys came to call on Lucky, bending under the always open doorway to enter. Much to their surprise, they saw Lucky and the author absorbed in the little Golden Books. They made a quick, curious assessment of the scene, quietly tipped their cowboy hats and slowly backed out of the house with slightly strange expressions on their faces. This soft side of the rough and tough image of Lucky's life may have surprised the equally tough cowboys.

Not far from Lucky Whidden's property was the historic tourist attraction on U.S. 27, Tom Gaskins Cypress Knee Museum. In 1999, Tom Gaskins, after a long battle with the State of Florida, had to dismantle the Museum workshop and move his family to Transylvania near Venus. He was evicted from a life time lease based on a hand-shake agreement between Tom Gaskins, Senior and Charlie Lykes, Senior. The lease was not honored after Charlie Lykes, Senior passed away. The long-time Cypress Knee workshop and Museum made with tall cabbage palm trees was left to return back to the Earth. The author was there on the last day when Tom Gaskins, Jr. loaded the kilns, old Cypress knees, and equipment from the workshop onto a flatbed truck. What remains outside behind the workshop is the treacherous two board, boardwalk and wire grip that loomed over the creek with Gaskins' characteristically named Cypress Knee statues implanted in the swamp along the walkway. Lucky Whidden was one of the Palmdale residents who fought with other locals and the Attorney General to keep Fisheating Creek open as a "navigable waterway" during long legal battles. Lucky took the battle a step further when he lit an acetylene torch and cut down an obstruction on the river that he claimed had been purposefully felled to block the navigable waterway. The long-time heyday of the Cypress Knee Museum and the dismantling of hand-carved welcoming signs along U.S. 27 announcing the approach to the Museum are now all gone. What remains today is the old sour Orange tree right outside the old workshop that produced big juicy oranges. Gaskins enjoyed offering tourists one of the big oranges from the tree and watching them pucker-up when they took a deep bite into the bitter, sour orange.

What remains of the Museum along U.S. 27 across from the workshop is now taken back by Nature with only a snarly view of this bygone era of Native Florida history cherished by so many in Palmdale and visitors from around the world.

Today, however, there is a new generation of pioneers such as Greg Johnson living in Palmdale. Fortunately, after living there awhile, he met Preservationist Ellen Peterson (now deceased) who offered him a job as "Caretaker" of the little house she built at Whidden's where Johnson lives today. Ellen Peterson, for many years, managed the Fisheating Creek Campgound. After Ellen's passing, Johnson purchased the property in 2006. Ellen Peterson was the founder of the "Save our Creek" organization that still exists today to protect the pristine wilderness threatened by creeping urbanization. Johnson is also a Preservationist and member of Save our Creek. He continues to preserve the native Beauty of the land just as Lucky Whidden and Peterson did for many years before him.

Similar to Whidden's maverick lifestyle, Johnson likes the rough life, the "outlaw" image of living in a little-known place on the edge of the wilderness and surviving in Nature. He has carved out a life like the early settlers in the 1800s who poled down the Creek, delivered mail, fished and hunted in the woods and along the banks of Fisheating Creek, or drove cattle through Florida into the vast Palmdale landscape settling with their families into a lifestyle of living off the land.

When Johnson discovered the stories of Palmdale through his explorations of Florida and the 1990's the fight to save the Creek. Johnson adopted a personal mission to preserve the Creek in its natural state, and to introduce others to an appreciation of its Beauty. He climbs tall oak trees to take town old liquor bottles hanging over branches left by campers who swing from ropes into the creek. He and other young Palmdale residents, Doug and Christopher Kelley join him in keeping trash removed along the creek and hike the area looking for debris to clean up Johnson is fortunate to have very supportive parents who encourage his alternative lifestyle. Johnson said his mom wanted him to pursue a college education but he did not want an inside job; he chose to live and work outdoors. Johnson's parents recognized his dedication to live off the beaten path in Palmdale and helped him to renovate Peterson's wooden cabin with essential necessities to live there.

By choice, Johnson bathes in a bucket of fresh water from a pitcher pump outside the cabin on a wooden table, where he also rinses his dishes after cooking over an open fire or on a small gas stove inside. The cabin is lined with solar panels that provide minimal light, hooked up to cable on the floor to a car battery and inverter box. He has no noisy electrical appliances or refrigeration, only a cooler. Outside he has a pile of firewood for camp fires, cooking, and warmth.

Johnson's says, "Kids today don't know how to grow a garden or do minimal labor. We need to teach young people that as a survivalist some day you may not have a house and will have to live off the land." As one of his Nature hobbies, Johnson takes lots of pictures and shares them with others he reaches out to in his urban travels. He shares his love of the land and stories about his lifestyle with those living in landscaped suburbia.

For a social life, Johnson remains friends with Arcadia buddies and continues to expand his realm of friendship to all he meets along the way. He enjoys socializing with Palmdale neighbors over a good fresh cooked meal at the newly revived Palmdale Cracker Store exchanging adventure stories and wildlife tales. Johnson offers his help to other residents and shares his knowledge and perspective on what he has learned living "off the grid." Johnson is reviving the spirit of early America returning to a Native lifestyle, living his dream, and creating his own legend as a 21st Century wilderness man.

EIGHTEEN

THE REVIVAL OF THE LEGENDARY PALMDALE STORE

APRIL 2016

After 16 years, the Palmdale Store has re-opened as the "Palmdale Cracker Country Mall and Social Club;" the only restaurant and convenience store for miles around in the heart of beautiful, pristine Glades County.

The new General Manager, James Sprague and his wife, Beth, discovered Palmdale when they decided to move from Fort Lauderdale. "We began our search for a more rural area in which to live and work. Driving north on U.S. 27, I saw a 'Cook Wanted Sign' posted on the old Palmdale store. I contacted Larry Taylor, the owner, we met and he hired me," said Sprague. Taylor also owns South Dixie Truck Sales down the street and has fought many years through grandfathered zoning trials and tribulations to re-open the store.

"Over the past three years I opened and managed three Fort Lauderdale delis and served as Executive Chef. When I got this job," says Sprague, "I moved to Palmdale with my wife and other family member to begin re-furbishing the Old Florida landmark. I am focused on re-creating the legendary Old Florida atmosphere of the store and restaurant, featuring country-style cooking and specialty dishes. I hired five other employees elevating Palmdale's population from about 300 residents to 562. The Palmdale Cracker Country Mall and Social Club, I discovered is the perfect rural location to start over. But Beth and I decided we needed to come up with a new name for the restaurant that reflects more than just a fast food eatery and convenience store, thus, we came up with the new name."

Many locals have always met at the store to eat and socialize when it was previously opened and now everyone can gather and enjoy a delectable menu and relax in the breeze on the beautifully remodeled cracker porch.

"We first expanded the old front into a large breezy wrap-around "cracker porch" with wooden benches and dining tables, adding a touch of the wild with a beautiful McCaw parrot in an outside cage nearby," Sprague adds. "Besides the outdoor facelift, the Spragues' added additional shelves inside and stocked them with old time favorites from the days of Old Florida. Some of the specialty items include Orange Blossom honey, Guava jelly, Everglades seasonings and a favorite for kids of all ages, grabbing a hand-full of wrapped candy on the bulk candy aisle. There are sugary treats such as original salt water taffy, candy coated almonds, "Bits of Honey" filled with peanut butter, "Nick Nips, the old-fashioned wax bottles with colored sweet syrup, Tootsie rolls and Cracker Jacks with the prize inside, and, there is more. Sprague says not only does the store offer a unique dining experience; it has "a little bit of everything."

Above the wooden shelves lining the inside walls of the store, are original pictures of Palmdale's heritage "cow hunters" and their families who settled in Palmdale in the 1800s. The store stocks camping/fishing gear, hunting supplies, cattle, horse, and game feed for wild boar, deer, and turkey hunters.

Since the store re-opened in 2015, local area residents, long time former patrons, truck drivers and travelers along U.S. 27 have re-discovered a place in their heart and began to once again drop in and stay awhile. Long time Palmdale resident, Ray Hendry whose mom used to work at the long gone, Palmdale Hotel, sells homemade carved wooden benches displayed on the porch

Sprague had not stopped short of offering a wide selection of country dishes described on the menu including specialty items made to order such as Cuban coffee and sandwiches. The "Quick Start Station" offers help yourself homemade dishes including scrumptious chicken and dumplings, chili, cornbread, biscuits, cheese grits, locally grown collard greens and ham hocks and ice cream, guava pastry or cheese and coconut flan for desert. There is also a wide selection of drinks to choose from such as sweetened/ unscented tea, pop, beer and wine.

While visitors were browsing through the store, Beth Sprague was busy designing and painting a brand-new sign to be posted along U.S. 27 pointing the way for travelers find their way to the front doorstep. Comfortably lodged on the cracker porch, are three bikers from England exploring America were enjoying a refreshment stop. Bryn Thomas from United Kingdom, Kevin Horton and Simon Garnham from England wanted to know more about the story of the pioneer "cow hunters" and were looking at the book, "Where the Swallowtail Kite Soars – The Legacy of Glades County, Florida and the Vanishing Wilderness," by Nancy Dale, available inside.

The Palmdale Cracker Store and Social Club is open for breakfast, lunch and dinner, served 7 days a week, 7 a.m. to 7 p.m., Monday through Saturday, closing on Sunday at 3 p.m. On the weekend is the “Saturday Night Special” featuring local Palmdale entertainers who play a variety of country favorites for listening and dancing.

For a unique experience, delicious food and socializing with all those drawn to the legendary Palmdale landmark, The Palmdale Cracker Store Mall and Social Club is a revival of Old Florida.

NINETEEN

THE LAST STAND OF THE PALMDALE CRACKER COUNTRY MALL AND SOCIAL CLUB

OCTOBER 22, 2016

The final curtain was lowered Sunday, October 23 on the historic Palmdale Cracker Country Mall and Social Club as it smoldered into more than fifteen feet of ashes and debris from a fire that began early Friday morning, October 21st. As the fire peaked during the day, clouds of smoke and flames ravaged the store from 8:00 a.m. until 2 p.m. when Firefighters, on the scene, declared "the fire contained suffocating the lifeblood from the legendary store. During the two-day fiery rampage, flames poured out of second story windows blanketing most of Main Street in the tiny community of 590 people. The beloved gathering place of Palmdale residents and thousands of others, whose fortuitous path led them up the wooden steps of the Cracker Porch and into their hearts forever, is now Legend. On Saturday, the remaining vestige of the beautiful wrap-around wooden Cracker Porch remained somewhat in tack after the interior was gutted until as if released from the Gates of Hell, the fire smoldered again into flames. Bob Jones, Director of Public Safety and Glades County Fire Department said, "when there is low heat and humidity there can be a flare up." On Sunday, the Cracker Porch, a popular gathering and dining place for residents and weary travelers to relax, succumbed to its destiny.

The original Palmdale store opened in 1928 and was the only store for miles around. It was a welcome break for truckers and motors traveling the long haul over 20 long miles on U.S. 27 between Moore Haven near the bottom of Lake Okeechobee north to Venus and Lake Placid. For residents, the store was much more. It was a favorite gathering place for the community that they called "home."

The disastrous fire flared up early as General Manager, James Sprague, was preparing the Friday Fish Fry, making brownies, and setting up the kitchen. "It smells like something is burning," Sprague said to his assistant, Kathy, "then I looked out the back door and saw flames soaring from the upstairs windows. I grabbed a fire extinguisher and ran up the stairs. I told Kathy to get out and I started rescuing the parrot and birds off the porch, the money, Lotto tickets and everything I could grab. Larry Taylor, the owner arrived a few minutes later as I was beginning to get dizzy and eventually was overcome by smoke. After what seemed like 40 minutes, the Moore Haven Fire Department arrived. According to Bob Jones, Director of Public Safety and head of the Glades County Fire Department said they "received an emergency 911 call at 8:14 and arrived at 8:28." Jones said "I was present as fire trucks from around the community arrived to fight the fire with 60,000 gallons of water, enough to put out the fire. We also established a water line into Fisheating Creek as we know that Palmdale does not have a good water source needed to suppress a fire but we had more than enough water. Until about 2004, Palmdale had a Volunteer Fire Department as Fire Fighters were not required to take certification courses but in 2016 the State of Florida instituted new training regulations," says Jones. Palmdale does not have any certified Volunteer Fire Fighters or a Fire Department.

The official statement updating the crisis came through the Glades County Emergency Management Administrative Assistant, Marisa Shivers in a New Release to the Media. "Glades County Sherriff's Office Dispatch was notified on October 21, 2016 at approximately 8:00 am that flames could be seen from the second story window of the Palmdale Cracker Store. Moore Haven Central District was paged out and arrived on scene soon at 8:28 per Bob Jones. "It was discovered that the second floor of the building was fully engulfed. EMS Station 3, Buckhead Ridge Fire Department and Ortona Fire Department assisted. Mutual Aid was called with Clewiston Fire

Department, LaBelle Fire Department, Felda Fire Department and Lake Placid Fire Department. Emergency Management was on scene to assist with responder relief and called in the American Red Cross to assist with a displaced tenant. The State Fire Marshall will be investigating how the fire started. The flames were contained by 2:00 p.m. The structure was a complete loss."

THE REMAINS

"In 2016, the State passed new requirements to become a Volunteer Fire Fighter with a 206-hour Fire One Certification training course. The County provides this training free of charge including books and use of all the heavy training equipment. We have people taking the course ranging from ages 62 to 18. It is preferable to live in Palmdale, but we do hire people from the local area to work in Palmdale. Most of the training is performed in Moore Haven. We need at least 4 to 6 people signed up to train in Palmdale as it might not be feasible to haul all the heavy equipment and materials to that location to teach the course with 1 or 2 people. We will work with those who receive certification to assist them in finding a fire truck to create a Volunteer Fire Department. The Fire One Certification includes a 40 hour First Responder's course, Wildland Fire Training and an Emergency Vehicle Driving course. If someone is not able to pass the physical requirements for the Fire One Certification, they can take the First Responders Course or Wildland Training portion and become part of the Brush Division where only First Aid is required should it be needed to administer to an injured person. The Fire One Course lasts 6 months, meeting Tues/Thurs and ¾ day on Sat." Those interested in becoming a Volunteer Fire Fighter in Palmdale can contact Bob Jones between 8 – 5 pm., Monday through Friday at 863-946-0566.

Marisa Shivers of Emergency Management states that "we have 3 certified Fire Fighter trainers in the county and offer classes often. We are presently doing a class in LaBelle. We offer these classes free and have for years. We just advertised it in the paper and have Glades County citizens enrolled in the class. The community needs to get involved and have a meeting to see if they have enough people to join and take the required training. If they are not willing to do these steps then the volunteers will have to continue to come from other communities."

However, back in Palmdale as news of the store's demise spread, local residents and motorists started to trickle into the remains of the burnt structure. As flames still smoldered and smoke filled the air, people stopped by to talk and remember "the good old days."

Larry and Marisa Taylor, the store owners struggled over 16 years to re-open the store overcoming many obstacles. Then in 2015 it happened. Taylor and Marisa re-opened the store hiring James Sprague as General Manager. James Sprague and his wife, Beth, discovered Palmdale when they decided to move from the Davie area. "We began our search for a more rural area in which to live and work. Driving north on U.S. 27, I saw a 'Cook Wanted Sign' posted on the old Palmdale store. I contacted Larry Taylor, the owner, we met and he hired me," said Sprague. Taylor also owns South Dixie Truck Sales down the street and has fought many years through grandfathered zoning trials and tribulations to re-open the store.

"Over the past three years I opened and managed three Fort Lauderdale delis and served as Executive Chef. When I got this job," says Sprague, "I moved to Palmdale with my wife and other family members to begin re-furbishing the Old Florida landmark. I was focused on re-creating the legendary Old Florida atmosphere of the store and restaurant, featuring country-style cooking and specialty dishes. I hired five other employees elevating Palmdale's population from about 300 residents to 562. The Palmdale Cracker Country Mall and Social Club was a perfect rural location to start over. But Beth and I decided we needed to come up with a new name for the restaurant that reflects more than just a fast food eatery and convenience store, thus, we came up with the new name."

"We first expanded the old front into a large breezy wrap-around "cracker porch" with wooden benches and dining tables, adding a touch of the wild with a beautiful McCaw parrot in an outside cage," Sprague adds. "Besides the outdoor facelift, the Spragues' added additional shelves inside and stocked them with old time favorites from the days of Old Florida. Above the wooden shelves lining the inside walls were original pictures of Palmdale's heritage "cow hunters" and their families who settled in Palmdale in the 1800s now destroyed by fire. The store had just celebrated its one year re-opening anniversary before the fire took its toll.

Long time Palmdale resident, Ray Hendry, born in Palmdale whose mom used to work at the long gone, Palmdale Hotel, sold homemade carved wooden benches displayed on the Cracker Porch. Fortunately, the benches did not succumb to the fire and he was able to haul them to safety on Saturday.

Alice Yates, who worked at the restaurant and is mother-in law of James Sprague and mother of his wife, Beth, relocated to Palmdale to work at the Palmdale Cracker store. "We really love this little store, the community, and the town of Palmdale. We plan to remain in Palmdale now as residents and hope we can all find jobs because the fire left our family with $0 income. We have made a lot of new friends here and love them dearly. I will truly miss seeing all of their faces every day," Yates added.

Ray Hendry's son, Ray Jr., recalls his own endearing memories at the store. "In my childhood and in recent times I would sit in the store after having ice cream and a glass bottle Coke and watch my father (Ray Hendry) and boys playing with the metal puzzles that were always at the store that nobody could figure out. I sat with my family eating dinner after work laughing and conversing. There was always a Bible on the table. Those memories will never be forgotten and my boys Allan and Tucker Hendry will never forget the times they got to spend in that store with their parents and grandparents." Going through some of the rubble on Saturday, a burned Bible was saved as residents gathered around to appreciate its retrieval from the ashes.

Gatorama owners, just down the highway, Patty and Allen Register, also have fond memories of their experiences at the store along with other friends. "Joyce Gillett, long time Palmdale resident worked at both the Oasis, now returned to the Earth, and the Country Store. Joyce told me chuckling that she had a fun memory at the store of drinking a Margarita with friends. I told Joyce I didn't think they served Margaritas at the store; she said, 'They don't so I brought my own!!'"

Allen Register added his own fond memories when Dick and Sharon, owned the store and had a cockatiel sitting on the counter by the cashier. Allen said that "the owners made the best gizzards in the world sold at the store."

Patty Register added, "I appreciated being able to get supper down there after working all day if I was just too tuckered out to cook. The renaissance of the store was something that Glades County was proud of; it gave us renewed Hope. The store was part of the DNA of this community. I appreciated Larry Taylor taking a chance on the community with his business plan. He tried to find the store's merchandise niche. It was a difficult situation. We certainly can never replace the Store's place in this community. Just like the Oasis, it's a landmark gone but the stories will live on for at least a couple more generations."

"As a young man, it was a big event to go to the Palmdale Store," says longtime resident, John Farabee. "It was like going to a big city coming from Venus." I will always remember those days." Arriving in his refurbished antique car, Bill Harris from Buckingham and Dave Pilly held their antique car meetings at the store and expressed remorse over their loss of a friendly location.

As the Palmdale community gathered at the ruins, there was discussion of "revival." A hastily composed Palmdale Store Revival Committee took shape; the sign outside the store was revised to attract attention of motorists on U.S. 27 with the announcement of an upcoming fund raiser and discussion of a truck annex to the store selling food. However, Larry Taylor, heavily grieving over the loss is not yet ready to commit to reviving the store. James Sprague and Ray Hendry suggested to Taylor that they could start over with a food stand in front of the store. Larry Taylor said to Hendry that maybe they could call it the "Firecracker" annex.

At the present, Hendry and the community are working to clean-up the remains and give Taylor time to recover before any future plans are made. Hendry did say, however, that he and others would be attending the next Glades County Commission meeting to ask for help in reviving the Palmdale Volunteer Fire Department.

One thing for sure, the Palmdale residents determined, and resilient to rekindle the legendary store in whatever form it may take in the future. If there is Hope for a new beginning it is in the hearts and minds of the Palmdale community. Just as the sign posted on the Cracker Porch says: "Thank you for your visit friends. Go with God and return soon."

TWENTY

"WHAT A DIFFERENCE A DOG CAN MAKE: SHEBA"

THE FOUNDING OF THE PETER PAUL POWELL MUSEUM OF ART

GUEST CONTRIBUTOR: FRED LEAVITT - CURATOR

AVON PARK

It all started with a therapy dog named Sheba. On Saturdays, my wife Gail and I took our therapy dogs to visit residents in nursing homes. I never expected it to change our lives and the cultural landscape of Highlands County.

We were at Sunny Hills Assisted Living Facility in Sebring and invited to roam the halls visiting patients in rooms with open doors. My dog Sheba led me down a long corridor and entered a room at the far end.

What immediately grabbed my attention was the number of oil paintings crowding the small room. They were stunning, timeless, images of Central Florida.

I heard Sheba talk, a real crowd pleaser, and looked at the patient. He was slumped over in an overstuffed chair. He was oblivious to his surroundings. Sheba went to plan "B" and put her head in his lap. That did it. The man became aware and he smiled.

The man was Peter Powell Roberts, a Florida Master Artist. He was an instructor and department head at the Ringling College of

Art in Sarasota for 23 years. After retiring he moved to a homestead adjacent to Highlands Hammock State Park and painted the Hammock environment full time.

He painted on wood pallets made in a variety of shapes. His focus was on the hammock minutia and often overlooked underbrush that gives birth to the beautiful flowering landscapes other artists are attracted to. His talent resulted in a body of work that reflects nature in the near-abstract. This work had a profound influence on Florida art history.

When his wife of 46 years died, he lost his anchor. Peter and his work went missing. He went into depression and was found penniless two years later.

Peter came alive when Sheba put her head in his lap. We became friends and I visited him several times a week. The remainder of his paintings and eight sculptures were recovered later in a metal storage shed.

Although he had chronic obstructive pulmonary disease (COPD) and Diabetes he started painting again. One of his paintings was put up for sale and immediately sold for $10,000. His passion returned and he painted continuously until he fell ill with pneumonia.

When he died in 2014 at the age of 88, he left his work to the Heartland Cultural Alliance (HCA), a not-for-profit organization, of which I am President. HCA is dedicated to advancing the arts and culture of Highlands County. We are determined to preserve and exhibit this valuable collection rather than selling it. The vision was to create a museum that served the community, attracted tourists, added to the cultural assets of Downtown Avon Park, and the economy of Highlands County.

May 18, 2016, we opened the Peter Powell Roberts Museum of Art and Cultural Center in Avon Park, Florida. The Museum is a showcase for his art, as well as a learning center and quality venue for Florida art in its various forms.

This includes the sculptures and furniture made by artist John Claytor from the rare, sunken logs he salvages from Florida rivers. The Museum is now drawing people from all over the country to the rural community of Avon Park. It took a remarkable chain of events and people to make this happen. I believe they were planned, but not by me.

TWENTY ONE
"SUNKEN TREASURE"

GUEST CONTRIBUTOR: CYNTHIA MCFARLAND

Previously published in the June 2016 issue of Ocala Style Magazine. Used with permission, ocalastyle.com

"How one local resident explores Florida's waterways to harvest centuries-old timber"

By Cynthia McFarland

There's got to be an easier way to make a living. Actually, there are thousands of easier ways. But for John Claytor, none of them offers the challenge and satisfaction that he finds in harvesting long-lost sinker logs and turning them into unique pieces of furniture.

Logging has long been recognized as one of the world's most dangerous professions. Add the daunting element of underwater recovery and you've got "deadhead" logging, one of the most difficult, labor-intensive timber job you can find.

John Claytor wouldn't have it any other way.

With a reputation second to none in this unusual field, the Ocala native recovered his first underwater log in 1970 and has been a full-time deadhead logger since 1999.

Nationwide, there are probably fewer than 100 people doing what Claytor does. His wife, Cathy, helps with the bookkeeping end of their business, Deadhead Logging, while his son, John Jr., also assists. Claytor refers to him as the "computer guru."

Deadhead logging isn't about pulling fallen trees out of a swamp or river. It's a whole lot more involved than that. And for clarification, these loggers aren't going after trees that just fell in the water but, rather, sunken logs and timber that have already been cut, most of them over 100 years ago.

Back in the late 1800s, when Florida was much more "wild and woolly" than her civilized 21st century self, the peninsula was covered with abundant stands of old growth longleaf pines and swamps boasted massive giant cypress trees, some thousands of years old. All that natural wealth attracted the attention of logging companies eager to turn timber into cash.

After the daunting accomplishment of felling the trees with axes, the loggers then had to transport the enormous logs to a saw mill. Before the railroad, the fastest way to move the hand-cut logs was by water.

"The logs were cabled or chained together and floated downriver to the mill," Claytor explains. "Sometimes the logs weren't dry enough to float and would start to sink, so the logger would cut it loose and sacrifice one or a few to save the rest. That's how many logs were lost."

The Florida Department of Environmental Protection, which claims ownership of most logs because they are located on sovereign submerged lands, estimates that about 10 percent of cut trees sunk during the transport process. Once on river bottoms, the lack of oxygen and cool, tannic waters did a remarkable job of slowly preserving the lost timber over the decades.

It's not certain how or when someone recovered the first deadhead log and realized how versatile and valuable the wood they yield is, but now they're highly regarded and can bring as much as 10 times the price of conventional lumber. Their tight grain, durability, resistance to rot and impressive color range make the submerged logs truly unique. Making them all the more desirable is the fact that they're limited—and hard to come by.

"They call this product 'pre-harvested timber.' This is a non-renewable resource; when this wood is gone, it's gone," says Claytor. "Today, it's become popular to use reclaimed wood from old buildings, but the rarity, strength and beauty of this river wood makes it even more valuable. There's so much time, effort and money that goes into getting it."

Hitting The Water

"Getting it" is precisely what fuels Claytor. His passion is obvious as he shows the fruits of his labor and talks about the challenge of finding sunken logs, let alone recovering them. Fit and athletic, Claytor's physical condition and sharp wit belie his 67 years, but his work-worn hands are a testament to the dangerous and exacting work he does on a daily basis.

In 1965, Claytor was just a junior at Lake Weir High School when he started scuba diving in Florida's rivers. On his dives to find arrowheads, old bottles and other antiquities, he kept noticing fallen logs. He asked around and found out a few people were trying to salvage them and sell the lumber. Claytor decided he wanted a piece of the action of this resource that could never be duplicated.

After a short stint in the Army, Claytor became a manager for mobile home plants. For many years, that remained his main job while he pursued his underwater logging business on the side. By the time he was ready to log full time, Claytor had become a master of finding and recovering submerged logs. Modern technology has enhanced the methods of reclaiming sinker logs.

“When underwater logging started, you either had to find them in shallow water or, if the water was clear enough, you could look down and see them on the bottom. In the early days, we found them one by one,” he recalls. “Now, technology has stepped up the treasure hunt. We’re finding logs we never would have found before without experience, knowledge of where to look and learning how to use technology. Some of those logs are buried several feet below the river bottom.”

Claytor utilizes side scan sonar to identify whether or not the object under water is a tree or a pre-cut log, meaning it was harvested at one time. As he explains, it’s illegal to take a tree that fell into the water on its own. He can only take pre-cut trees that were harvested before the current laws were established. In other words, he's "re-harvesting" trees someone else harvested—and lost—many decades ago.

Half the battle is knowing where to look, a skill that can only be mastered with time and experience.

"It pays off to do your research," says Claytor, who has logged over 10,000 underwater hours. "I always look for old saw mill sites because you often have a good chance of recovering logs that were lost or left behind. It wasn't uncommon for a mill to close when money or help ran out, and they just left, often leaving wood behind. I've found several places in the Suwannee River with hundreds of logs. In Dunnellon, I found an old mill site in the corner just above the bridge where the Blue Gator is now. I pulled hundreds of heart pine logs out of that spot; they were stacked 25 logs deep.

"At one time, Wilson Cypress on the St. Johns River in Palatka was the largest producer of cypress in the world. This was around the late 1800s and early 1900s. I researched this and found thousands of board feet of cypress logs and boards there. Murphy Creek just south of Palatka is another spot where I've gotten great logs out of an old mill site."

Some of those were "extreme" logs, meaning they're more than 30 inches in diameter and 30 feet, or longer, in length.

The Legalities Of Logging

Just being in the water to search for deadhead logs requires multiple steps beforehand.

Claytor had to be certified as a master deadhead logger, sign a use agreement with the state, plus apply and pay for multiple permits. He's also required by state law to hire an archeologist who goes to the state master file in Tallahassee and researches his permitted areas. If the archeologist finds that an area may have sites of historical value, Claytor is prohibited from logging in that specific part of the river. Many water bodies, such as springs, are completely off limits to loggers.

"There are 13 agencies that have laws affecting my business," says Claytor, adding that all of his logs are legally recovered from Florida rivers. "You can't just go out there and harvest old wood. I have to get a state permit every year and a separate permit for every 20 miles of river stretch I operate in. Right now I have over 200 miles of permitted stretches of water that I'm working."

Locating the submerged logs is only the first step. The next challenge is removing them.

Using a set of grapples—they look just like a huge set of old ice tongs—on one of his four boats, Claytor dives down and hooks onto the log. Then he uses the barge to pull and break the log loose, which isn't as simple as it sounds. With some logs, it literally takes days to work them free of the mud and silt on the river bottom.

"Once we get it free, we 'stage' it, which means we get the log to the shore and put a buoy on it with my permit number, just like you'd have with a lobster or crab trap in Florida waters. The state tells us where we can take logs out of the water; we either have to own the site or have written permission from the land owner or the state, if it's state land," says Claytor. "After we get logs to the staging area and stock pile them there, we bring a truck and trailer to pick them up and transport them to where they're going to be stored or milled. There's a lot of handling before you get ready to cut a log, let alone build something out of it."

Unfortunately, on occasion, people—call them "log rustlers," if you will—steal logs out of the staging area before Claytor picks them up. When that happens, all his hard work is for naught, but there's not much he can do about it.

From Log To Lumber

Once the massive logs, some of which weigh 8,000 pounds or more, are in his possession, Claytor must have them dried before he can do anything with them.

Cypress holds an astonishing amount of water. Claytor notes than 1,000 board feet of cypress will contain 310 gallons of water before being dried. This is best done by placing the milled wood on sticks and letting it air dry, but you can't be in a hurry. It likes to dry slowly; 1 inch of thickness takes about one year to dry. Pine, on the other hand, is kiln-dried. Claytor says it takes anywhere from two to four weeks for heart pine boards to dry down to a moisture content you can work with. (Keep in mind this is not the same pine you'll find at your local lumber store. This is from old growth longleaf pine, and there are only a few thousand acres of virgin old growth pine left in the country today.)

In the past, Claytor sold the dried lumber to carpenters, homeowners and woodworkers. Then about a decade ago, he decided to use it himself and started making his own furniture in his second business, Water Wood Originals.

As if salvaging this remarkable lumber wasn't enough, now

Claytor makes one-of-a-kind furniture, each piece with its own distinctive history and guaranteed authenticity. Anyone who buys one of his creations gets the entire history of the wood he made it from, something you can't get at one of the "big box" furniture stores.

"I love the thrill of the hunt of finding logs, but I also get a lot of satisfaction from making a unique piece of furniture that someone can incorporate into their home and enjoy," says Claytor, who has 30 years of saw mill experience on the old mill he bought and rebuilt on his property. "When you mill this lumber, it's just like the day the tree was cut down. You're getting the same piece of wood the man who cut it down 100 years ago was hoping to have. It's like opening a box of Cracker Jacks and getting the prize.

"There's no limit to what you can dream up with this material," adds Claytor, who just finished redoing his own kitchen with cabinets made from cypress milled from logs he salvaged from the Ocklawaha River.

When crafting a piece of furniture, Claytor likes to leave telltale signs of the wood's history, such as the axe-cut end on a heart pine bench. "Axe cutting stopped around 1890, so anything you find axe cut was harvested prior to that. Then they went to two-man saws," he notes.

The edges of one table made from cypress displays the unique pattern left by ship worms, which eat the outside of the tree. Claytor finds cypress with this unusual appearance predominately in the salt and brackish water of the St. John's basin.

In addition to stunning tables, benches, shelves and stools, Claytor also makes intricate carvings from heart pine, the hardest medium of wood to carve, thanks to its high pitch and resin content.

His workshop is brimming with things he's found underwater over the years, including shark's teeth, ancient bottles, arrowheads, fossilized mastodon and mammoth teeth. One of the most curious things he ever found was a copper moonshine still discovered on the bottom of the Suwannee River.

Anything he finds of historical value, Claytor donates to schools, museums or historical societies so the people of Florida can benefit. The moonshine still, for example, was donated to the state and is on display in Tallahassee.

Although many men his age have quit working and are spending their days on the golf course or pursuing hobbies, Claytor has no interest in retiring.

"I'm still working as hard or harder than I've ever worked. I'm scared to retire," he laughs. "I've acquired a lot of knowledge, and I want to continue putting it to use. I feed on leaning, and I love finding out about new things."

No one can be sure how many deadhead logs lie submerged in Florida's rivers, still waiting to be salvaged. Claytor knows there's a limit to the number of logs out there, and that, someday, they'll be gone. Until then, he has every intention of staying in the hunt.

Learn More › deadheadlogging.com › waterwoodoriginals.com

TWENTY TWO

THE AMAZING STORY OF THE HISTORIC CYPRESS KNEE MUSEUM

1930-2017

PALMDALE

Twenty to ten thousand years ago when the last Ice Age began to retreat, straggly haired hunters wearing the skins of their trophies crossed over Berengia, the icy land bridge from Siberia, tracking giant mastodons to the bottom of the Earth into the peninsula of Florida. When the Paleo-Indians of the late Pleistocene Epoch migrated to Glades County, it was barren and dry unlike the lush cabbage palm prairies and cypress swamps that exist today. But, all that remains of the ancient ones' struggle to survive the unpredictable, unforgiving natural forces of the Everglades are fossilized bones, giant animal skulls impaled with spears, and mound villages scattered across Glades County.

Since those ancient times, many explorers have made their way to Glades County and survived. Some pioneers paddled their way down Fisheating Creek in hand-carved canoes, rode atop hand-sewn leather saddles, traveled the rails of the Hinky Dinky or drove shiny black Tin Lizzies on muck-rutted trails, each bringing with them their satchel of dreams.

In the 1900's, Otto Fog laid out his plan to create a "Garden of Eden" in Palmdale. At the center of the town was the picturesque Palmdale Hotel with verandas sporting tall silk hats atop groomed, dapper tourists on the arm of ladies clad in egret feathered bonnets, satin dresses gracing wide-open porches reaching over tannic cypress swamps. What remains of those dreams and the majestic hotel are a few wooden pine frames wrought together by hardened sap and rock, unmarked, unknown.

Those pioneers who survived the hurricanes, droughts, black clouds of mosquitoes, cottonmouth moccasins, rattlesnakes, alligators and the swamp, learned to live in harmony with the land that gave them life. There is no other place on Earth like the pristine wilderness of Glades County. The whispering fans of tall cabbage palms, ancient cypress trees grabbing the ceiling of the Earth, and Fisheating Creek meandering through the heartland, become "one" with those who linger here as long as time allows.

10-YEAR BATTLE TO SAVE FISHEATING CREEK - 1989-1999

"THE LIGHT OF DAY"

In this tiny crevasse of the vast Everglades spectacle, a living image unfolds on Nature's palette that captures the senses and stamps its unique imprint upon space and time. There is a raw serenity here that shingles the spine and rekindles the spirit of the secret observer mingling in the shadows beneath the outstretched moss-laden arms of a solemn oak. And it is here, in the last wilderness area of Florida that the citizenry of a small town with undaunting courage and relentless spirit initiated a legal battle against a multi-international corporation to save Fisheating Creek as a public waterway. Palmdale, on the edge of the Everglade's prairie, a town of some 300 citizens took on Lykes Brothers.

PALMDALE VS MULTI-INTERNATIONAL LYKES BROTHERS, INC.

The property dispute between the State and Lykes Brothers had its roots in the 1980's. Lykes Brothers claimed that they, not the State, owned the portion of Fisheating Creek that ran through their property in Palmdale. A handful of 300 + determined Palmdale citizens challenged Lykes Brothers to preserve the heritage of Fisheating Creek as a navigable public waterway through their property.

In 1989, the battle between the people of Palmdale and Lykes

Brothers peaked. For many years, Lykes Brothers allowed access to Fisheating Creek and several fishing holes on their Palmdale property. In 1989, Lykes barred public usage of the creek and posted inimical signs along the edge: "NO TRESPASSING. FISHEATING CREEK IS A NON-NAVIGABLE STREAM AND TRESPASSERS WILL BE PROSECUTED, Lykes Brothers." Palmdale residents took their case to Attorney General Bob Butterworth.

In the meantime, as legal actions were pursued in the court, some restless Palmdale residents pursued other "outlaw" measures. On Christmas Eve of 1989, Palmdale resident and descendant of pioneer ranchers, Lucky Whidden, boldly took an acetylene torch to the steel barricade Lykes Brothers posted a barricade across the creek to block passage. In another incident, Smiley Hendry and his son were arrested for allegedly trespassing, cutting fences on Lykes property and assaulting a Lykes Brothers security guard. Becky Hendry (a Hendry County namesake), founder of "Save the Creek, Inc." and wife of Smiley Hendry, refused any plea agreement from Lykes' attorney and insisted on going to trial or having all charges dropped. The charges were summarily dropped.

According to David Guest, formerly of the State Attorney General's office, employed by the Earth Justice Legal Defense Fund, the original lawsuit filed against Lykes Brothers in 1989 sought an injunction to immediately remove the posted signs on the creek that declared it was not a navigable waterway. Attorney General Bob Butterworth based the lawsuit upon the 1823 Florida Act declaring that all navigable rivers in Florida must remain forever public. Tampa Federal Court Judge Elizabeth Kovachevich dismissed this suit on September 22, 1989 ruling that there was "no jurisdiction" under the statute.

A second lawsuit filed by Attorney General Bob Butterworth was based upon the Rivers and Harbor Act of 1890 prohibiting activities that affect rivers without obtaining a permit from the Corps of Engineers. This suit was the result of Lykes felling trees across the creek to block passage on the stream. Tampa Judge Kovachevich again dismissed the suit and issued an opinion that it was up to the Corp of Engineers to determine if Fisheating Creek was a navigable waterway. Attorney General Bob Butterworth filed another lawsuit to demand a "navigability determination" on Fisheating Creek from the Corps of Engineers.

The dispute between Lykes Brothers and the State caused conflicting interests for the citizens of Palmdale. Some residents worked many years for Lykes Brothers and were afraid to jeopardize their livelihood, especially in a county that ranks near the highest in unemployment and near the lowest in per capita income in Florida. But the townspeople united, held meetings late into the night searching through old Florida books, memories, historic records and albums for hardcore evidence that Fishing Creek had been navigable as far back as the 1800's.

1800'S – BILLY BOWLEGS HUNTED GATORS IN THE CREEK

One old Florida book that turned up included a recorded account of

Seminole Chief Billy Bowleg's gator hunting along Fisheating Creek in the 1800's. Chief Bowlegs (Cho-fee-hat-cho) spoke of paddling from Lake Okeechobee to camp at Palmdale, poling across Rainey Slough to the Peace River watershed and down the river to sell hides and obtain groceries. Also discovered in another existing journal was an account of an 1842 Naval expedition that traveled down Fisheating Creek in the dry season in twelve, 30-foot canoes with sail and rudder. These historical records provided additional evidence in the case supporting the navigability of Fisheating Creek.

Ancestral Florida Indians the Calusas, the Yemasees, and "Mikasukees" called Fisheating Creek, "Tlalklapopka-hatchee." Early Seminole Indians (a Creek word for runaways) used the Creek as an escape route from the U.S. troops during the Seminole wars in the 1800's. Rock slabs in Fisheating Creek near Lakeport are the remains of Ft. Center where Seminoles were captured for bounty after the war. Homesteading pioneers depended on the Creek for transportation, trading and a mail route to other towns sprouting up on the inland waterway.

On Feb. 1, 1990, the Corps of Engineers issued its findings: Fisheating Creek was navigable. Following the release of the report, an attempt to attain Lykes Brothers concurrence that Fisheating Creek was a public river was unsuccessful.

In April, 1990, Lykes took the Corps to court. Two years later, July, 1992, Judge Kovachevich set a bench trial in Ft. Myers that coursed the summer of 1992. At the end, Judge Kovachevich issued a post-trial memorandum, ruling that even though a dugout canoe could cross from Okeechobee to Palmdale, it did not prove that the stream was "navigable." In September 1993, a fourth suit was filed based upon the river being publicly owned under State law. The trial was set for April 22, 1997.

A QUESTIONABLE VICTORY

On June 2, 1997, after a six-week jury trial under Circuit Court Judge Charles T. Carlton, a verdict was returned in 1-½ hours, ruling that Fisheating Creek was indeed a navigable waterway belonging to the State. In Dec. 3, 1999, the case was settled.

Represented by Florida Attorney General, Bob Butterworth, the Earth Justice Defense Fund, The Environmental Confederation of Southwest Florida and "Save the Creek, Inc.," the town won a lawsuit and property settlement agreement against Lykes Brothers, one of the largest property owners in Glades County, an international shipping magnate, citrus king and pioneer cattle barons. The settlement agreement was finalized December 3, 1999 after a ten-year legal harangue that established a wilderness area of more than 42,000 acres along historic Fisheating Creek flowing through the heart of Palmdale and Lykes Brothers property. Lykes brothers own approximately 82% of Glades County, which ranks near the bottom of per capita income in the state and near the top of unemployment in the State.

The State of Florida paid $46 Million to Lykes Brothers for

property on, and surrounding Fisheating Creek designated as a Wildlife Management Area. Lykes Brothers abandoned their claim to 9,000 acres of State owned land on the Creek. The State purchased an extended corridor of another 9,000 acres adjacent to the riverbed for designated recreational use and 42,000 acres (eventually 120 thousand acres) for a conservation easement to be maintained as an environmentally protected area.

THE END OF THE CYPRESS KNEE MUSEUM

However, there was one hitch in the settlement agreement. Tom Gaskins, Sr., who founded the Cypress Knee Museum along former State Road 25 (now Highway 27) in the 1930s, formerly owned by Lykes Brothers now belonged to the State. Tom Gaskins, Sr. and his then young family, lived on the Lykes owned land since the 1930's based upon a hand-shake agreement between Tom Gaskins, Sr. and Charlie Lykes, Sr., one of the original seven Lykes brothers. The proof of a legal written deed entitling Gaskins Jr. and family to remain on the homesteaded property after Gaskins, Sr. and Lykes, Sr. passed away could not be established or secured. Tom Gaskins's livelihood, the historic workshop and home was threatened by the events that occurred when Lykes Brothers' decided to shut down Fisheating Creek.

Scattered cypress knees line the entrance to the Cypress Knee Workshop in Palmdale

According to Tom Gaskins, Jr., the hand-built cypress tree residence of Tom Gaskins, Sr., the cypress knee workshop, and the unique hand built cabbage palm home would have to be relocated as well as his family, either across U.S. 27 next to the Museum that Gaskins owns, or to his other property in Tasmania, ten miles north. However, the Settlement Agreement between Lykes, the State and Gaskins threw out the question of who owns the handmade cypress structures on the property.

Uncut cypress knees left sculptured at the close of the Cypress Knee Workshop

Part of the State's settlement, claimed sections of Lykes Brothers property on both sides of U.S 27, including the residential homestead of the deceased Tom Gaskins, Sr. on the East Side of the highway, across from the Cypress Knee Museum he founded in the 1930's. When old State Road 25 became U.S. 27, the property where Gaskins Sr. lived was split down the middle. The Cypress Knee Museum was located on the west side of the highway; the residence built by Tom Gaskins, Sr., the cypress knee workshop/catwalk, and the cabbage palm residence built by Gaskins, Jr. was east of U.S. 27.

The hand-built cypress tree home of the Tom Gaskins, Jr. family – Palmdale

EVICTED

On November 4, 1999, Lykes Brothers, on behalf of the State of Florida, ordered Tom Gaskins Jr. to vacate the property by December 3, 1999, the closing date of the property settlement; Gaskins did not vacate. On February 16, 2000, an "Eviction Notice" was filed by Lykes in Glades County Court. The Complaint stated that Lykes was withholding their consent for continued possession of the property effective December 3, 1999.

On May 3, 2000, a motion to transfer the "Eviction Notice" case to Hendry County was granted by Judge Keith Cary who scheduled a jury trial in his court June 7, 2000. The complaint, filed by Lykes Brothers, delineated an action to recover possession of unlawfully detained real property located in Glades County, Florida under Section 8201 of the Florida Statute. The complaint asked for damages (back rent) and possession of the property. The complaint stated that Gaskins Jr. did not pay any rent on the property while living there since the l930's.

Tom Gaskins, Jr. said there was a boundary dispute and attempted to negotiate a land trade with Lykes and the State to remain on the property. The regional Historical Society recommended to the State that the Gaskins' homestead be registered as a National Historic Site. However, Tom Gaskins, Jr., whose wife had been diagnosed with cancer and undergone two major surgeries, wanted to resolve the conflict as quickly as possible. In lieu of a trial, he said he would re-locate the historical residence to his property in Venus (Tasmania). The historic 1930's homestead of pioneer Tom Gaskins Sr., the Cypress Knee workshop and cabbage palm residence of Tom Gaskins, Jr. was about to become another disembodied landmark in Palmdale's ragged history.

THE FATE OF A PIONEER HOMESTEAD

"The Agreed Final Judgment" on two, of three remaining lawsuits by Lykes Brothers against Tom Gaskins, Jr. that relinquished all rights, title and interest or claim to the real property upon which the Tom Gaskins, Jr. family has been residing for more than forty years, was settled. Lykes brothers conveyed the land to the State of Florida December 2, 1999 subject to the contractual duty of Lykes to clear title and deliver possession of the land to the state. When Tom Gaskins, Jr. did not vacate the property by the closing date of the Lykes/State of Florida property settlement agreement, an eviction notice was filed by Lykes in Glades County, and then moved to Hendry County, for a jury trial originally scheduled for June 7. However, in lieu of the mediation to negotiate an agreement that was ongoing between Lykes attorney, Bert Harris, Gaskins Attorney Kenneth Jones, a Mediator and The Nature's Conservancy, a non-profit organization, the trial was postponed. The last remaining unsettled lawsuit that attorneys refrained from providing details, involved the Cypress Knee Museum property on the west side of U.S. 27, across from the Gaskins homestead.

The "Agreed Final Judgment" delineated that the "personal property and improvements situated on the land (including all buildings and their respective contents, but excluding all trees and growing things) are the property of Tom Gaskins Jr. and Billie Jo Gaskins, husband and wife. Plaintiff Lykes makes no claim upon Gaskins' personal property. Lykes waived and relinquished all claims for rents, profits, and damages against Gaskins pertaining to the Gaskins' use and occupation of the land. Defendants Gaskins shall file for any and all variances needed to utilize their Venus (Tasmania) property for the Gaskins personal property on or before June 9, 2000. Should it be necessary for the variance request to be considered and decided by the County Commission, the Gaskins' shall diligently pursue such application so as to have the variance request scheduled at the first legally available County Commission meeting. The Gaskins' shall remove the Gaskins' personal property from the land within 90 days of the final administrative decision on the variance by the Planning and Zoning Commission or the County Commission, whether such decision be a granting or denial of the variance. Any portion of the Gaskins' personal property remaining on the land after the above deadline shall be deemed abandoned by the Gaskins and shall become the property of the State without further action, order of judgment." The judgment was approved and agreed upon by all parties, and filed in Hendry County June 8, 2000.

Attached to the "Agreed Final Judgment" was the "Mediation Agreement." Attorney James Nulman acted as the mediator between Lykes Brothers and the Gaskins family with all parties meeting in the Ft. Myers, June 2nd, 2000. The mediation agreement involved the relocation of Gaskins personal property (all buildings and contents) to Tasmania part of Venus, north of Palmdale off U.S. Highway 27. An additional clause in the Mediation Agreement stated: "Should it be necessary for the variance request to be considered, Lykes hereby agrees that neither Lykes, nor any Officer, Director, employee, or representative of Lykes, shall in any way oppose or object to Gaskins' application(s) for such variance(s) to utilize the Venus (Tasmania) property."

Further stipulations of the Agreement: "Lykes is entitled to entry of the "Agreed Final Judgment" upon proof that $75,000.00 to be paid by the Nature Conservancy into Gaskins' Attorney, Ken Jones Trust Account. The parties agree to equally divide and pay the Mediator's Fees, one half being paid by Gaskins and one-half by Lykes. A counterclaim by Tom Gaskins and Billie Jo Gaskins was dismissed against Plaintiff Lykes, with prejudice."

"The Nature Conservancy will pay $75,000 towards the cost of moving the Gaskins' personal property from the land to the Venus (Tasmania) area in Glades County. The escrow agent, Attorney Ken Jones will disburse the trust funds to the vendors relocating the Gaskins' personal property upon written certification by The Nature Conservancy that the for expenses related to moving Gaskins expenses are approved. The trust funds shall be used exclusively to move the Gaskins personal property to Venus (Tasmania) or such other property as the Gaskins' select in the event the permits and variances are not obtained for the Venus (Tasmania) property. Such expense includes such items as, but is not limited to, permits, variances, infrastructure, moving the structures and other personal property. Any funds remaining in the trust account not utilized for authorized relocation expenses shall be repaid to The Nature Conservancy."

Elthea Stafford, Director of Glades County Planning and Zoning Department indicates that the removal of the personal property of Tom Gaskins' homestead (the cabbage palm residence of Tom and Billie Jo Gaskins, the cypress knee Workshop and original hand built Cypress home of now deceased pioneer Tom Gaskins, Sr. falls under the "Family Homestead" guidance law meaning Gaskins does not have to apply for any variances from the County Commission or the Planning and Zoning Department in order to re-locate his belongs to his property in Tasmania. Since the settlement agreement with Lykes Brothers and the State of Florida in December, 1999, to provide more than 60,000 acres of land for a Wildlife Management Area along Fisheating Creek, Gaskins was evicted from the property in a final mediation agreement between Nature's Conservancy, Lykes and Gaskins Attorneys settled June

6th, 2000 (Gaskins could not prove the existence of a deed to the property). The mediation agreement allowed Gaskins 90 days to obtain any variances, if required, in order to remove all of the personal property to his approximate twenty acres of land in Tasmania.

Ms. Stafford outlined the stipulations of the Building and Zoning Codes and explains that the Family Homestead law allows Gaskins to move the property to the new location, but forever after, he cannot sell any the property to anyone other than a family member. Gaskins only needs to apply for the appropriate permits, and complete all requirements prior to the permits being obtained. After permits are obtained with construction drawings completed, and inspections authorized, then the power can be turned on at the new location. According to Brian Prowant, Environmental Specialist with the Glades County Health Department, the clock started ticking June 9th, on the 90-day removal period of the personal property, the date he issued the septic tank permit for the new location.

THE FINAL DAYS OF 1999

The Gaskins' family had already begun to pack up the Cypress Knee Workshop piece by piece on pick-up trucks, until the final day when the huge caravan of 1930's historic residential structures would travel down U.S. highway 27 to its final destination in Tasmania.

Evicted! Palmdale's historical Cypress Knee workshop is loaded onto truck.

After forty-years where three generations of Gaskins' lived, all that is left behind is the old plank boardwalk circling the swamp where the 50-year-old cypress knee sculptures will be taken back into the Everglades. Coke bottles sucked into the bark of the growing knees will never be seen again. And the sour orange tree that Tom

Gaskins' Sr. used to tout to the tourists was "the sweetest orange in Glades County," would stand-alone in the vacant spot that used to guard the entrance to the workshop. Tourists can still remember the laugh as they took a bite out of the bitterest native orange they ever tasted. The personality of the man, the Museum, and the art will soon disappear forever from this homestead.

Larry Campbell, of the Division of Fish and Wildlife Conservation Commission, the agency designated as the managers of the new Management Area was asked if there were any plans for the State to construct another catwalk, or other structures on the Gaskins homestead property when vacated, but he said there were no plans. Today, the property is encased in a steel fence and the two-planked catwalk is being taken back by the swamp.

2000 – THE GASKINS' HOMESTEAD LOADED ON FLAT BED TRUCKS

As the nation celebrated its birth on July 4th, 2000, the Tom Gaskins' family prepared to move Palmdale's historical landmark, the 1930's homestead of Florida pioneer Tom Gaskins, Sr.'s handmade Cypress workshop, residence and Gaskins, Jr.'s cabbage palm structured house to Tasmania, near Venus.

In the pictorial display in the center of the book, Tom Gaskins, Jr. described, in his own words, "a soon to be lost art." "My personal feelings are one thing and having lived with this place (the Cypress Knee Museum and homestead established by Tom Gaskins, Sr. in 1937) for 59 of the 64 years it has been here, puts it close to my heart. My personal feelings aside, to see a place as true and genuine to old Florida ripped to shreds by the State that just twelve years ago conferred upon it the 1987 "Heritage Award," tells me that the left hand doesn't know what the right hand is doing in Tallahassee. Governor Bush could have solved this problem, and he knows about it full well know this. But he chose to remain aloof. If you ask me, it was insane to do this.'

"My father developed many skills sculpturing Florida cypress knees that he passed down to me and I was beginning to pass on to my sons when Lykes Brothers cut us off from cutting Cypress knees ten to twelve years ago. At one time, it was a very happy arrangement, but new people came on the scene and things changed."

From Left to Right: Jim Gaskins, Tom Gaskins Jr. and Tom Gaskins, III

Billie Jo expressed her appreciation for all of the support friends have given the family, in letters, faxes and kind notes. Billie Jo, who survived breast cancer surgery during the ordeal, conveyed a gracious and generous smile as she expressed her gratitude "I can't put into words how much I appreciate the barbecue benefit at Hendry's Sabal Palm Campground, and all of the people who came out to offer the family support all the way from Palmdale to Tallahassee." Billie Jo said they were ready "to move forward with their lives, but is sad thinking about what the State and Lykes Brothers have done do the historical site." The homestead, when re-located to Tasmania will not be open to the public.

THE MAN WHO WORE NO SHOES

The life of Tom Gaskins Sr., the founder of the Cypress Knee Museum, embraces the true Florida "cracker" spirit. In the early 1900's, Tom Gaskins, Sr. and his son passed through Palmdale from Arcadia and often stayed at the Palmdale Hotel. In 1937, he settled in Palmdale and began a mail-order business selling handmade turkey callers and Cypress Knees. He cut, skinned and sold the cypress knees to taxidermists for mounting everything from birds to bears. For $1.00, he invited tourists to visit the Museum and take a daring catwalk that still swings precariously from Cypress trees above the swamp behind the workshop on the East side of U.S. 27. He enjoyed the look on visitors' faces, including the author's, when he offered a taste of a wild (bitter) Florida orange from the tree outside the workshop.

"Tom Gaskins, Sr. the original founder of the Cypress Knee Museum at Palmdale as born in Tampa, March 26, 1909. He was raised in Arcadia and graduated with the Class of 1927. He worked with and was a salesman for Gator Roach killer until 1934 when he married Virginia Bible and started the cypress knee industry. In 1937, they moved to Palmdale where they lived in a house covered with about 30,000 hand-split cypress shingles, everyone he made. In 1947, he invented, manufactured and started selling his unique and nationally famous wild turkey callers. The Cypress Knee Museum opened in 1951. At age 69, he still jogged eleven miles, barefoot, every day through the Cypress Knee swamp along Fisheating Creek, near the old Moore Haven road grade behind his house. Gaskins, Sr. called himself a woodsman, hunter, fisherman, and woodcarver. He held ten patents for inventions during his lifetime" (*Florida Facts and Fallacies, by Tom Gaskins,* 1978).

Tom Gaskins, Sr. established his Museum on the Tin Lizzie Trail to Palmdale, when old model-T's took "a day or two to travel 50 miles but it was faster than horse or horse and wagon." Since there were no motels in Florida's early days, people pitched a camp on what was called "pine islands" or high ground, although by the 70's Gaskins claims that much of the water was drained, leaving armadillos and ditches. Gaskins' book, publishes many "Florida cracker" wisdoms, a term he declares has a debatable origin. Either the Florida cracker gained reputation from the cow hunter's s quick crack of their whip, or from a North/South battle in North Florida when crack shots were credited to Florida Crackers. Today, a "Florida Cracker" is referred to a native, born and raised in the State.

The Everglades, since time memorial is identified with the jagged-edged saw grass and the cypress tree. Cypress trees generally grow in low areas where there is a lot of water. Cypress trees that string out over miles, is called a "cypress strand." Behind the Gaskins' residence was a vast cypress swamp with long cypress strands that still exists today in Palmdale providing a shaded canopy along Fisheating Creek.

According to Gaskins, Sr. "the only tree that has knees is Cypress but all Cypress do not have knees. Cypress knees grow up from the roots of the tree and have no leaves, no limbs, and they do not make a tree. Gaskins thought knees stored water for the tree during dry weather, or to aerate roots of the tree during high water, or were an evolutionary left-over when it was a protective device like a thorn." The theory best liked by pioneer Gaskins was "one supplied by a visitor, toothpicks for dinosaurs!"

The sculptured Cypress knees are natural, but undergo a simple process invented by Gaskins, Sr. to enhance its beauty. Normally cypress knees are solid. When Gaskins began to cut and peel them he saw the opportunity to make things out of them and sell them. He first advertised cypress knees in House and Gardens Magazine in November 1935. He has a patent on the manufacturing of them since 1937.

Tom Gaskins Sr. carves cypress knee

At the Cypress Knee Museum, he had a collection of knees from twenty-three states in a vast variety of forms. Usually the knees grow up straight, but then Nature becomes creative. In the museum, Gaskins had one called a "Lady Hippopotamus Wearing a Carmen Miranda Hat." One last walk through the cypress swamp, along the hand-made catwalk behind the cypress knee workshop, the progress over twenty years of natural growth, evolved a different and unique sculptor from the original description carved on the sign, posted on the earlier date, soon to be taken back by the encroaching Everglades habitat when left on its own.

What will not disappear is the original craft passed down by apprenticeship from Gaskins, Sr. to Gaskins, Jr. and his sons: The sculpturing of the raw Cypress knees into objects of art. The process is long and precise. The tools often hand-crafted by Gaskins, Sr. from everyday utensils. The old chair, which became a part of Gaskins Sr.'s life for more two-thirds of a century remains, and one can feel the frame of the man molded into the back of the two Cypress limbs where the sculptor spent his life working with nature's mysterious cypress knees and artistic imagination to create lamps, tables, mounts for birds and bears for all those who passed through the portals of his workshop. The woven lampshades, handmade from palms, the polished statutes, some hovering over five feet, lined the workshop in various stages of completion.

Before the flatbed trucks arrived to carry them into an unknown future, the wooden floors were scattered with pieces of knees waiting in the dust and an attic stowed the last cargo. If the art will be revived is not known, but the skill of the unique craft will forever be the inheritance of Tom Gaskins Jr. and his two sons, Tom III, and Jim.

2004: THE EVERGLADES RECLAIMS ITS OWN

The State erected a fence around the property where Tom Gaskins' used to take his daily barefoot run in the swamp, crossing the old railroad bed that one time carried cypress trees to the lumber mill. That too is only a rusted, overgrown memory. There is no monument from the lives carved out of the Cypress forest. Even the old Museum across the road is sinking into the sand, unattended and uncared for. A legacy has disappeared in Palmdale and only those who watched Tom Gaskins and his sons carve the clocks, the lamps and turkey whistles will remember what used to be, every time that empty spot is passed along the highway. Nature left the old sour orange tree to stand guard by the limestone path that carried millions of footsteps into the wilderness.

2015: REVIVING THE CYPRESS KNEE MUSEUM

On May 12th, 2015, Glades County leased the Cypress Knee

Museum from the Department of Environmental Projection as part of the Division of State Lands for 30 years to preserve it. According to the Lease Agreement, Lessee shall manage the leased premises for public related venues that may include the establishment and operation of the Cypress Knee Museum including the related Cypress Knee Museum uses hat have historically occurred; he establishment and operation of tourism related uses, including tourism development uses and welcome center uses; Glades County government and quasi-government uses, including economic development uses and Chamber of Commerce uses; public outdoor activates nod education activities and other related uses necessary for the accomplishment of this purpose as designated in the Management Plan. The leased premises shall not be developed or physically altered in any way other than what is necessary for security and maintenance of the leased premises with the prior written approval of Lessor until the Management Plan is approved.

According to Glades County Manager, Paul Carlisle, "Glades

County is the lease holder. A group of volunteers has developed a conceptual plan to look at opening a Welcome Center. No true plans are in place at the present time."

Tom Gaskins, III said he would "like to see the museum site repurposed/restored into a Glades Welcome Center (either Glades County or broader 'Everglades" region.) Part of the purpose would be to remember the Cypress Knee Museum and the work that my grandparents' and parents did there. I see it as a place people could view a pictorial history of the county and region among other things. I would also like to see if the Russ Smiley mural, currently covered with graffiti, could be restored. Currently Glades County has leased the property from the State and has submitted a management plan that is awaiting approval. "

"As former Chair of the Fisheating Creek Settlement Agreement Advisory Board, I am very glad that Glades County Government has signed a lease in order to protect Cypress Knee Museum from demolition, and I hope that this historically important former roadside attraction will someday be restored for the benefit of the people of Florida and its many visitors.

APRIL 2017 - THE REMAINS OF THE CYPRESS KNEE TODAY

These pictures show the present state of the Museum when visited by Palmdale resident, John Farrabee and the author. John Farabee remembers the Museum: "Before Interstate 27 was a major highway to Miami and other tourist attractions, the Tom Gaskins' family literally carved out a place in history. Tom Gaskins, Sr. collected Cypress Knee from Illinois, Pennsylvania, New York, Texas, Delaware, North and South Carolinas, Georgia, Oklahoma and many other states. The family always had ties in Palmdale and many friends. He had a love for Cypress on a sand hill in Palmdale. I can still envision old Model T's traveling on this road. Thousands of people discovered this unique attraction and were able to take with them a handmade Cypress Knee lamp or the famous "turkey caller." Maybe the future will bring the revival of his historic landmark."

JOHN FARABEE, PALMDALE ON OLD STATE ROAD 29

OLD ENTRANCE ON STATE ROAD 29

JOHN FARABEE POINTING TO CYPRESS KNEE LOCATIONS

JOHN FARABEE INSIDE

MAIN DISPLAY

CENTER PIECE OF OLD CYPRESS TREE

INSIDE GUEST HOUSE

GRAFFITI OVER ORIGINAL RUSS SMILEY MURAL

ORIGINAL HANDMADE SHINGLE ROOF

TWENTY THREE
THE UNTOLD STORY OF FLORIDA'S INDIGENOUS PEOPLE: THE BELLE GLADE CULTURE

LAWRENCE E. WILL MUSEUM OF THE GLADES

BELLE GLADE

Fourteen thousand years ago the Florida Everglades and much of the peninsula was wet and wild until after the last Ice Age 11,000 years ago when it began to dry out. When the peninsular started to thaw, the first human inhabitants began to settle around Lake Okeechobee in the Kissimmee River Valley. These first indigenous people were the Belle Glade Culture whose story was buried thousands of years beneath Florida's white sugar sand on the southeastern coast of Lake Okeechobee.

In the 1930's, a vault containing cultural treasures of these indigenous people was excavated from a mound on the Wedgwood Farm in Belle Glade revealing earthwork artifacts and pottery between AD 700-1500.

The Works Progress Administration (WPA), in partnership with the Smithsonian Institute, Washington, excavated the mound just outside the city where artifacts were discovered dating back over 3000 years. Over time, as other mounds were excavated the collection of pottery, shells and bones increased and are now housed at the Lawrence E. Will Museum in Belle Glade, Florida.

After studying the artifacts, archeologists identified the Belle Glade people as a large population of foragers, hunters, and gatherers. The exhibit at the Lawrence E. Will Museum of the Glades have an archived collection from the Belle Glade Culture, artifacts of early Seminole Indians, Florida's pioneers, and relics of the 1960's. The Smithsonian Institute has also preserved some of the Belle Glade Mound collection. The County Historic Preservation Office also coordinates with Florida Atlantic University (FAU) bringing in interns from the Anthropology Department to assist with historic preservation.

The Belle Glade indigenous people, who survived through several archeological periods, now will take center stage at 5:30 p.m., Oct 6th, at a special "Town Hall Meeting" at the Museum to shed light on this remote, almost forgotten culture now preserved in perpetuity.

At the event, the Museum will provide an opportunity for guests to learn about this little known culture. Florida Gulf Coast archeologists/anthropologists, professors and students from the FGCU field study school will be on hand to answer questions. Hosted by archeologist, D. William Locascio of Florida Gulf Coast University, the public can dialogue with him and those who studied the artifacts.

"The Town Hall Meeting" will engage the community and other stakeholders in learning about the archeological field work investigations conducted by FGCU at the site," says Dorothy Block, Director of the Museum and Professor of Archaeology at

Palm Beach State and Broward Community College. Little known facts will be unveiled, spotlighting the lifestyle of a people that Profess Blocks says "were very similar to Florida's modern Homo Sapiens.

At the Town Hall Meeting, Professor Block and other archeologists will reveal little known facts that will "surprise people." At the meeting, everyone can enjoy refreshments, study the artifacts, and talk to professors as they bring the past to life through their scholarly interpretations.

Lawrence E. Will, the namesake for the Museum, was the son of a Glades pioneer who conducted his own research around the Lake and published **what he learned. He also operated** freight, passenger and towboats in the early 30's.

The present Museum is located at the site of the former Belle

Glade Library and became a reality through the efforts of Professor Block, founder of the PB Archeological Society and the community. The Museum was incorporated in 1976.

The Lawrence E. Will Museum is located at 530 S Main St, Belle Glade, FL 33430 - Phone: (561) 853-4443

TWENTY FOUR

UNSUNG ADVENTURER: CAPTAIN F.C.M. BOGGESS

DESOTO COUNTY PIONEER

ARCADIA

A rugged Florida pioneer who wrote his own destiny fighting in 4 legendary Wars from Mexico to the little known Spanish-American War in Cuba of the 1800's, Capt. F.C.M. Boggess leaves behind a living legacy honored today through the lives of his Arcadia, Florida family.

On one beautiful afternoon, the legacy family of Capt. Boggess, gathered around several large tables on a sunny screened porch overlooking an unspoiled pond at the homestead of Barbara Collins whose husband's family lineage dates back to Boggess, as well as the Kinards, Jim Brewer and Sowells. It was an afternoon of laughter and stories about the adventures of a man who lived a rugged individualist life, as commemorated in his autobiography plucked out on an old ribbon typewriter and published in 1900. On this lovely day, the family opened their lives with vivid historical memories, pictures of Boggess, and their own heritage homesteading along the beautiful Peace River dating back to the 1800s.

Asena Mott, Jim Brewer, Selby Kinard,

Barbara Collins, June Sowell

According to the Boggess autobiography, his family emigrated from France, eventually settling in Madison County, Alabama during the Armed Occupation Act that attracted new settlers to the area. Frances Calvin Morgan Boggess was born in Huntsville, Alabama, Nov. 21, 1833 that he says was marked by "a grand meteor shower. My parents spoke only French but to survive learned to grow cotton, raise horses, cattle, and sheep." Eventually, young Boggess pursued other plans. F.C. M. Boggess, saw his first steamboat in Alabama and without much thought climbed aboard; its destination, Mobile. With little money and no friends, he followed an inner-calling for adventure. Young Boggess had high aspirations when he received some education but then was recruited by a Colonel to join a U.S. battalion involved in the Mexican-American War of 1846. The Mexican cavalry attacked and killed a group of U.S. soldiers under the command of Colonel Zachary Taylor in a border war along the Rio Grande. Boggess' recollection of the scrimmage was one of dramatic survival "nearly dying from dysentery, pulling packed mules through rugged terrain, struggling through marshes, and guarding mountain passes from guerilla attacks until peace was declared and the Stars and Stripes hoisted on a snow-top mountain."

Boggess's adventuresome spirit spurred him onward after the Mexican War. Thousands of discharged soldiers were at a loss to earn a living and "were ready to engage in anything no matter how dangerous," says Boggess. His next encounter was as an Officer in the American forces focusing on the Cuban rebellion against Spain.

In 1850, American troops prepared to make sail to Cuba. Upon preparing to board the steamer, *Creole,* Captain Boggess' regiment was riddled with bullets as the 4,000 man artillery troops did not arrive. Eventually, says Boggess, "some troops were sent back to the U.S. to prepare for more attacks. The regiment eventually scattered and Boggess returned to Florida.

Around 1817, when the Seminole Indian Wars began in Florida, Andrew Jackson was making excursions into Creek lands of West Florida initiating conflicts that lasted through 1858.

In 1858, Captain Boggess settled into a more reserved lifestyle in Polk County, teaching school, hunting cattle and participating in cross-state cattle drives to markets in Punta Rassa near Tampa and the east coast in Fort Pierce. Eventually, Captain Boggess married had children and moved to the Peace River in DeSoto County that was rich in Phosphorous. The family eventually branched out into the living legacy of Brewers, Kinnards, Sowels and Collins.

As the beef industry expanded in Florida, the Collins family raised cattle along the Peace River which provided a port for shipment. In those days there were no fence laws and Jim Brewer, said "cows were trained to come home; they didn't need fences." But he adds, "Life was rugged in those days. There was no electricity, people grew their own food and killed hogs to survive." Barbara Collins said giving birth was also difficult as "they only had midwifes to deliver children. June Sowell said, "It was a hard life in those times and difficult to survive disease." Cindy Collins added, "There was only one Doctor with a specialty in Botany, Dr. Aurin, who was reliable in finding natural remedies for some illnesses. Yellow jaundice, which affects the liver, was treated by Dr. Aurin with a batch of locally grown herbs." But, Barbara Collins says that despite rough conditions, "childhood was a happy time on the ranch. Children grew up playing on the River and discovering ancient artifacts such as Shark Teeth fossils from prehistoric times." Asena Mott, Director of South Florida State College in Arcadia and granddaughter of Barbara Collins, says her family has found numerous ancient relics with her daughter designing beautiful art pieces from many of them.

Made with shark's teeth Shasta Mott found in the Peace River

The legend of the Peace River is rich in many colorful tales. Jim Brewer says "one interesting folklore story is the pirate, Jose

Gaspar or Gasparilla hiding gold in the River. "Friends and I explored the River looking for the buried treasure. We discovered some possible clues but could not find it. However, I believe the gold could still be there!"

Today, members of the Boggess family legacy gather frequently repeating old stories over iced tea and homemade cake. Boggess' adventuresome stories are a tradition passed on to children and grandchildren and have a "life of their own." The family is a living legacy of Florida and the rugged pioneer spirit.

Jim Brewer, Barbara Collins, Asena Mott, June Sowell, Cindy Kinard, Selby Kinard

TWENTY-FIVE
"THE BOCA RATON RESORT & CLUB WELCOMES THE TASTE OF WALDORF ASTORIA"

GUEST CONTRIBUTORS: ELAINE AND SCOTT HARRIS, SOMMELIERS LAS VEGAS, NEVADA

The Waldorf Astoria Boca Raton is a part of history. It was an important link in winter luxury train travel for the affluent in the north east wanting to winter under the warm Florida sun. Go back in time riding in a luxurious private stateroom heading south on

Henry Flagler's railroad in the late 1920's and 1930's, leaving snow behind and the beckoning orange blossoms have you in anticipation of your upcoming winter activities.

The Boca Raton Resort & Club, which opened February 6, 1926 as the Ritz-Carlton Cloister Inn, is a large resort and membership-based club and one of the crown jewels for the elite on Florida's east coast. The luxury resorts included The Breakers in Palm Beach, Ritz-Carlton Cloister Inn, The Biltmore in Coral Gables and the Casa Marina (The Flagler Hotel) in Key West. Ladies and Gentlemen of the era enjoyed the best of the best at these resorts as the traveled the Flagler Railroad to Key West and some on to Cuba.

Arriving at The Waldorf Astoria Boca Raton took us back in time with unbridled luxury and service. This grand lady was originally designed by California-born architect, Addison Mizner in 1926. The Boca Raton Club Tower in was built 1969, the building is still considerably taller than any other building in southern Palm Beach County. The resort has recently undergone a $150 million renovation, while the cloister and tower rooms were redesigned in 2006.

The is located just a few steps from the stunning south Florida coastline and their private beach. Our wall to celling windows provided a romantic view of the Atlantic Ocean, Intercoastal Waterway and the marina which is the home of yachts well over 100 feet long.

Guests can dine at Dine at one of our 11 award-wining restaurants or unwind with the ultimate spa experience at the hotel's Waldorf Astoria Spa. Voted as the number one spa in the country by Condé Nast Traveler's Readers' Choice Awards. We were here on a culinary mission, The Taste of Waldorf that had us deep sea fishing and purveying ingredients with Resort Executive Chef

Andrew Roenbeck and James Beard rising star Chef Sara Hauman from San Francisco. The ultimate goal is to create some very special dishes paired with a cocktail and a mocktail to be presented in competition with other Waldorf Chefs at the Waldorf Astoria in New York.

In a world inundated by food TV contests and cooking competitions, an interesting twist on traditional rivalry is always a refreshing deviation into the creative culinary world. The Waldorf Astoria has partnered with the **James Beard Foundation** (JBF) for a third year to find the next Taste of Waldorf Astoria champion. Five JBF Rising Star semi-finalists have been individually partnered with one of Waldorf Astoria's Master Chefs for a multi-day collaboration to conceive the next culinary masterpiece. After the pairings have been created, the program culminates with a competition in February at the Waldorf Astoria in New York featuring a star-studded panel of judges who will determine the winning combination.

The **Waldorf Astoria Hotels & Resorts** have given the world classic dishes such as Eggs Benedict, Waldorf salad and the Red Velvet Cake and now there is a worldwide search for yet another dish to hallmark this iconic brand. Just before the holidays we joined two accomplished Chefs', one a twenty plus year veteran executive Chef of the Waldorf Astoria, Andrew Roenbeck and his counterpart a young James Beard rising star, Chef Sara Hauman of San Francisco. As Taste of Waldorf contestants, they must collaborate together executing a dish that could withstand the decade's recipe revelations, and unusual ingredients; a culinary challenge that propelled these chefs together without any prior communication as they were tasked to prepare a dish that will be not only featured in every Waldorf Astoria throughout the world but in the greater connection, an iconic dish is optimally going to withstand the test of time.

This year's contest: transform the happy hour into the "Fifth Hour" by expanding bar offerings beyond traditional drinks and appetizers. Roenbeck and Hauman were challenged to create two small bites that must pair perfectly with an original cocktail and mock tail. Working amongst themselves and the skilled Boca Raton hospitality staff, they carefully took several days in creating a truly memorable dining experience encompassing every detail from the overall presentation from plate to palate. We came along to catalog and chronicle the weeklong journey of these two vastly different chefs as they journeyed through their purpose, finding the best purveyors while developing their creative process into a winning plate of perfection.

Chefs Sara Hauman, left, and Andrew Roenbeck were paired to create the next iconic Waldorf Astoria dish.

The process of coming up with stellar recipe, especially one that is in competition to be in the food history books, was an educational and often adventurous journey as we traveled with the two Chefs on a week-long stint in south Florida. With several of us coming together from different parts of the country and various time zones, we were all a bit jet-lagged but ready to be educated on the flora and fauna of the surrounding area. We met with some of the best local purveyors in search for the superior ingredients needed in producing the winning menu items. Our first culinary assignment; meet at the Waldorf Astoria boat dock for a fishing trip. Living in the desert does not include fishing expeditions, so this looked like an intriguing adventure. The seas looked a bit choppy but knowing we were going to be with experienced fishermen, we put aside our doubts and bravely stepped into the small fishing vessel. Docked aside multi-million dollar yachts, this fishing craft looked diminutive and a bit fragile for the stormy weather that seemed to be brewing on the horizon. Our angst was starting to show, but we put on our seafaring faces and ventured into the channel as our jovial seamates reassured us of their skill and knowledge was all that were truly needed when the seas looked angry.

That seeming reassurance faded very quickly as large white caps loomed on the horizon. While the captain jokingly hummed the theme song to the 70's TV show Gilligan's island-(and we know what happened to that crew!) under his breath, we were thinking will our fate to be any different? His carefree attitude did not pierce our cloud of in trepidation as we heaved and pitched through from the inner coastal water way and into the Atlantic Ocean. We bounced through the thorough fare like a rubber duck in an agitated child's bath, all the while praying to the sea gods' for mercy. Once we cleared the channel our fate looked dubious as storm clouds and rough waters seemingly increased by the minute. Meanwhile hope glimmered briefly when the front fishing pole nearly bent in half sending the seamates into action; one grabbing the bowing pole and the other brandishing a menacing looking gaffing hook. The two worked in frantic unison bringing aboard the loveliest Mahi Mahi fish amidst bouts of bloody surrender, jostling and rejoicing. As the ill-fated sea creature flipped and flopped, our bodies undulated in the same frantic motion, as if to give some sort of sympathy dance as it was sacrificed for the cause. As our mission was now accomplished, we urgently implored the captain to turn the boat back to dry land, of which he obliged to our collective breath of relief. As we bounced back into the harbor we were relieved to have the first locally sourced protein in the Chefs quest for the best ingredients albeit almost to our own demise.

Chef Sara Hauman with her catch of the day.

The next day after a lovely breakfast we were on our way to meet a beekeeper and then off to a few organic farmers and a stop at a winery.

It's not every day that one is offered the use of a very expensive Maserati (the official town car of the Boca Resorts) as means of transport to a bee farm. Was it the warnings we were told beforehand that made us just a tad apprehensive? Such as, do not wear black, (what about the shining black Maserati that we were driving up in? Would that be the object of bee wrath), and make sure you cover your tootsies; bees love to get at your toes. Chef Andy reassured us that the bees were harmless as long as you adhere to the rules of the beekeeper. We soon were well versed on bee etiquette, as we entered into the buzzy world of Roxanne L. Altrui, passionate beekeeper. We gingerly opened the car door to the bee filled atmosphere; the distinctive buzzing sound and busy creatures were now surrounding us and we were anxious to approach their territory respectfully and safely. Roxanne, a tall robust woman adorned with a full bee suit, quickly gave us each our own suit and we made haste in getting our protective gear on as the bees were becoming increasingly interested in our presence. We felt snug and a much more relaxed in our protective garment, although a bit warm on this humid Florida day. Roxanne took us through an extensive overview of her bee world, with live demonstrations showing us the work of the queen bee to the birth of a new bee. Every facet of her work was fascinating and often enlightening. "See, there are millions of bees around us, and are they attacking us? No," she said, "they are only doing their job". And their job is making the incredible golden local honey that we came to gather on this day.

Bee populations in the area and in general are diminishing as unneeded spraying continues to kill off large number of these much-needed creatures. Roxanne claims to be the spokesperson for the bees and actually calls them her "girls "since there are no males. "We need bees to pollinate our food and they need us to help them thrive and dispel the fears that many people hold to be true often based in fear and ignorance", she added. Today we truly learned the beauty and complexity of the bee world and both Chefs procured the golden elixir for another ingredient in their menu quest. It was time to get back into our Maserati for the next part of our exploration.

Driving down dusty, palm tree lined roads with large open canals we lost our GPS signal. We knew we were truly lost out here in the brush of south Florida when we unknowingly happened upon the entrance to a nudist camp. Quickly turning around, our navigation system finally alerted us to farm known as Swank Specialty Produce operated by a husband and wife team, Darren and Jodi Swank.

Chef Andrew Roenbeck shows the honey he collected at the Apiary.

The couple is considered to be pioneers in the family farming business beginning in 2002. Hydroponic, natural farming was virtually non-existence and through a great deal of sweat, tears and extremely hard work the farm continues to offer the highest quality and best tasting produce in Florida. The Boca Resort was one of the first accounts for the Swank Farm. "Our products speak for themselves," said, M. Swank, "We were one of the first small family farms that started the local movement." Walking along the rows of brilliantly colored organic vegetables, we tasted fresh tomatoes, beans and other succulent organic produce. Both Chef Sara and Chef Andy seemed to bond over what produce that would be using in their next dish creation, and this place indeed seemed like a Garden of Eden, a perfect place to find the best ingredients. After waking the farm, it was time to visit a local winery and see what they had to offer up to please our palates.

David Bick, 42, and Teal Pfeifer, 33, are owners of the Palm Beach County's only winery; it includes a retail space and tasting room. As we entered the tiny tasting room we were looking forward in trying their wine made from dried hibiscus sabdariffa, also known as roselle, Jamaican sorrel, sour-sour and Florida cranberry. "This is one of the only organic ways to preserve a high quality product by making wine", claimed Bick. Bick and Pfeifer strive to maintain the organic purity of their product, and it comes out in the refreshing taste of this lovely coral color beverage that exuded subtle floral notes and an extra benefit we were told that although the wine boasts a 13% AVB, hang-over complications are nearly non-existence. The hibiscus wine now has a cult following, from well-known rock stars to enthusiastic locals and there is a waiting list as production is on a small family farm scale. We were fortunate to have a sip or two and to gather a few bottles for Chef Andy and Chef Sara's recipe treasure throve.

EPILOGUE

"BLUE GOLD: WATER"

The Earth is the only planet we know that survives by water. Eighty-percent of the Earth's surface is water, our brains 75 percent. As we grow older we "dry out" and become 50 percent water. Water is the content of our cells. Of the 11 gallons of water in the average body, 6 1/2 make up the fluid in cells. Water is the earth's thermostat and human body regulator of heat. Water stores heat and lowers body temperature. Fresh water amounts to 3.7 percent of the world's supply, mostly stored in glaciers, ice caps and the atmosphere. The limited amount of water available to human beings is drawn from wells, streams and lakes comprising .0007 percent of the global water supply.

Global water use has increased rapidly over the past 70 years. There are so many more people using water drawn from underground aquifers, artesian wells, rivers, streams and lakes that by 2025 at the present rate of consumption, 90% of the freshwater in developed nations will be used up. When fresh water aquifers near the ocean are pumped out, it is often replaced by saline water seeping in. Mammals and plants cannot survive with salt-water pollution in ground drinking water.

Besides a water shortage crisis, population growth and increased consumption degrade water quality available, contaminated by life-threatening substances including chemicals from industry, agriculture, and household products spilling into the fresh-water supply. Further, hormone and antibiotic laced animal and human waste seeping into storage basins recycling into human use, creates potentially devastating immune, endocrine and reproduction system disorders that only now, researchers are identifying as water related.

In Florida, sprawling golf courses "planted" in former orange groves are growing rapidly in the landscape of housing developments bearing namesakes that do not resemble their identity such as "Orange Blossom Estates," or "Cypress Hammock Community," with nary a fragrant orange or cypress tree in sight.

Golf courses with its chemical use to maintain lush greens are an environmental detriment, but golf is a big business contributing more than $49 billion a year to the U.S. economy. In the United States, golf courses cover more than 1.7 million acres and soak up almost 4 billion gallons of water daily. They also use pesticide and fertilizers that contribute to water pollution. In 1994, the University of Iowa's, College of Medicine, found an unusually high number of deaths from certain cancers among farm works and pesticide applicators working on 618 gold courses in the United States including brain cancer and non-Hodgkin's lymphoma.

The expansive population growth of 1,000 people a day moving to Florida that piggybacks on the number one industry of tourism and recreation is creating an expensive concern to solve environmental problems.

But the perpetuation of future problems is not contained in large urban areas as "sprawling transportation networks criss-cross the state creating new hubs of development extending north, south, east and west. The first step in re-structuring a rural community is through the development of a new economic infrastructure that provides services such as water, sewage treatment, roads to support industrial growth offering minimum wage jobs that promise a future by re-training rural workers, who may be only have worked as cowboys their entire life, into the "new economy" through job transition.

Moving along the urban coastal fringes like a bullet train towards Glades County is the threat of rural heritage and cultural extinction, including loss of wetlands, endangered species, and habitat, in exchange for air, water and light pollution. It is a high premium to pay for an urban-based economy.

A positive move in the current of events is that a few governmental groups in South Florida are discouraging the proliferation of urban sprawl. During the 60's and 70's, the growth philosophy of the urbanizing areas along the lower eastern coast of Florida was to accommodate growth by pushing development west toward the

Everglades counties virtually threatening to absorb rural populations of their distinct character and history giving way to auto dependent suburban residents. Although Glades County has only 1% of the land area utilized for urban land uses, with nearly two thirds owned by Lykes Brothers, growth issues from the east and west coast are already impacting the county with the addition of Governor Jeb Bush's Rural Economic Development Initiative (REDI) in 2000. The program provided funds for rural diversity including monies to determine if a county has the ability to provide infrastructure to support maximum projected growth under its existing comprehensive plan, or is the development for industrial sites ripe to turn from an agricultural or budding ecotourism economy into an industrial area.

The transformation of urban sprawl into what is termed "quality development patterns," is under the auspices of local governments, the South Florida Water Management District and the South Florida Regional Planning Council. The SFWMD and the SFRFC are representative of a board appointed to make decisions for the majority, in lieu of "by the majority" of people whose future lifestyle, economic stability, land/water use will parceled by their decisions.

In 2004, at Ortona, the Glades County Enterprise Zone Development Agency (EXDA) moved to generate more property tax per square foot by attracting industrial development, proposing more favorable future land use zoning. The proposal included changing a residential zone to industrial with the Governor's approval through the Office of Tourism, Trade and Economic development, not an "oxymoron" grouping of terms in the governmental office.

Funds available for tourism can be easily tied in with industrial development as indicated by the Governor Bush's office handling economic development. Enterprise zones are slated as economic areas targeted inside counties for industrial sites.

Facts to ponder: Water Usage in America

. 2 gallons to bush one's teeth each day

. 4 gallons to flush a toilet one

. 20 gallons to hand wash dishes; 13 gallons to put dishes through an automatic washer.

. 1, 800 gallons to refine one barrel of oil.

Water is life and we are the caretakers of the well. As water wears away the stone, and nurtures the creatures on Earth, it also is the first to "wither." When the land is turned to cement highways, trees cut down for development replacing indigenous species with ornamentals not adapted to Florida's unique climate the land and environment are altered, including evaporation and condensation of the water cycle.

When we lose intimacy with the natural world, cloned in air-conditioned cement block most of our lives, we become unaware and ignorant of the water related, live-giving processes we depend upon to survive. We then seem shocked, as if caught off guard when our insulated capsules are disturbed by a new culture that uproots and transplants the old ways and values, perhaps not in any better or familiar way, but more prolific and entrenched then life breath of the natural world.

Blue-gold water is the lifeblood of the planet that is non-sustainable and non-renewable ones it is siphoned from the Earth's stores before it can replenish itself through the natural processes of evaporation, condensation, rain and storage in the heart of the planets' reservoirs. Trees, plants and the habitat are all part of the water life cycle. The nurturing of life, blue gold water, exists as a non-sustainable and non-renewable entity when siphoned from the earth's stores before it can replenish itself through the natural processes of evaporation, condensation, rain and storage in the heart of the earth's reservoirs.

Besides the land, the blue-gold water that whispers silently over and through the underground primordial porous limestone beneath Glade's County is the custodian of life-giving forces. In the last of the vanishing wilderness areas in Florida, the wildlife cannot speak out, it is only the human guardians enjoy the pristine beauty, quiet and star clustered skies that have a voice in preserving Nature's wonders in a healthy environment.

Man, when surrounded by inanimate objects, becomes sterile. The mind and body replenish, just like the soil, the plants and other animals through the touch of Nature. Transcendentalist Henry David Thoreau became a symbol in his quiet revolution at Walden by rejecting society's "spin" on how he should live his life, thus, he grew vegetables instead of working in a factory. Though he attended Harvard University, he was an unconventional scholar as reflected in his life and writings, expressing a willed integrity to conscientiously refuse or accept the will of the government or others upon his own life direction and purpose. He believed in inner freedom and the ability for human beings to build their own lives. He was a supreme individualist and championed the human spirit against materialism and social conformity.

In 1845, he built himself a small cabin on the shores of Walden Pond, near Concord, Massachusetts to live in eloquent solitary and close harmony with Nature. He remained there for more than two years, "living deep and sucking out all the marrow of life." He supported himself by growing tomatoes, surveying and doing odd jobs nearby. He observed Nature and wrote about what he learned.

Thoreau expressed the rural values that are often dismissed today by those who believe in the dominant contrasting value of the "fast lane," chasing dollars, bigger and better, richer phenomena. Yet, when there is little breathing room, land and water left, replaced by ornamental, lifeless surroundings, man's sprit will evaporate just like the water. There are some intangible unsustainable life-giving forces that money cannot buy including, health, time and human relations.

Man's time is limited as are all creatures upon which we share this space in the universe. We are not alone, although we may seem alone. Our world is alive with the smallest and largest insects and beasts, from the tiny thriving anthill whose community has burrowed its nest in the Everglades sand, to the iridescent glow from a Florida black bear's eyes hollowing out shadows in the night in search of food. Imagine our world as we would make it: Sprayed lawns, cement houses, artificial lights, gated communities, traffic, pollution gray horizons, the smell of chemical fumes and the night so bright with lights that the stars die. What future do we choose to carve about how we choose to live?

"What is man without the beasts? If all the beasts were gone, men would die from a great loneliness of spirit. For whatever happens to the beasts, soon happens to man. All things are connected."

Chief Seattle, Suqamish Chief, 1859

THOUGHTS TO PONDER

"SILENCE"

By Greg

1979

The cool shade of the Evergreen tree falls

across the silent path in the woods,

Oh, what a nice feeling that flows right

down your spine.

Everything is asleep now except me.

The sun gets weaker and weaker,

Now it is gone to shine for some other place.

ABOUT THE AUTHOR

Nancy Dale Ph.D. is a Native Miamian, Author, Journalist, Adjunct Professor and Certified Yoga Instructor. She lives in Sebring, Florida.

"…. I have promises to keep, And miles to go before I sleep, And miles to go before I sleep."

Robert Frost, "Stopping by Woods on a Snowy Evening"

1923

www.nancydalephd@gmail.com or nancydalephd.com

Made in the USA
Columbia, SC
04 November 2019

82439978R00170